P9-AEX-440

Voices from Ancient Egypt

Oklahoma Series in Classical Culture

Oklahoma Series in Classical Culture

Series Editor
A. J. Heisserer, University of Oklahoma

Advisory Board

Ernst Badian, Harvard University
David F. Bright, Iowa State University
Nancy Demand, Indiana University
Elaine Fantham, Princeton University
R. M. Frazer, Tulane University
Ronald J. Leprohon, University of Toronto
Robert A. Moysey, University of Mississippi
Helen F. North, Swarthmore College
Robert J. Smutny, University of the Pacific
Eva Stehle, University of Maryland at College Park
A. Geoffrey Woodhead, Corpus Christi College, Cambridge/Ohio
  State University
John Wright, Northwestern University

R. B. Parkinson

Voices from Ancient Egypt
An Anthology of Middle Kingdom Writings

University of Oklahoma Press : Norman

To my parents

Library of Congress Catalog Card Number 91-7250

ISBN 0-8061-2362-1

University of Oklahoma Press edition published by
special arrangement with British Museum Press,
London. Copyright © 1991 by R. B. Parkinson
All rights reserved. First printing.

Voices from Ancient Egypt is Volume 9 of the
Oklahoma Series in Classical Culture.

Printed and bound in Great Britain

Cover and page 3 Painting of a scribe on an 11th-Dynasty model granary
(J. Bourriau, *Pharaohs and Mortals*, Cambridge, 1988, 86, 104-5).

Contents

Acknowledgements

My thanks are due primarily to W. V. Davies (British Museum) for suggesting this book. I owe a great deal to M. Smith and J. R. Baines (Oxford), with whom I first read many of these texts, and to the students with whom I have in turn read them. I must also thank S. Quirke (British Museum) for his advice on sundry papyri and his generous help; the various inhabitants of the Griffith Institute (Oxford); C. Klotz, M. Robinson and M-A. Newman for their editing and friendship; and my parents for their unfailing support. The text was finished in my first months at University College, Oxford, to whom I am greatly indebted.

Unless stated otherwise, the figures are photographs provided by the British Museum Photographic Service, and drawings by the author based on the primary publications listed in the bibliography. Several publications are reproduced with the kind permission of the Committee of the Egypt Exploration Society.

Introduction

'It is good to speak to the Future;
it shall listen.'

Despite these words of the sage Ptahhotep (see **15**),[1] the voices of the ancient
Egyptians cannot be recalled. All that remains are transcriptions in an
imperfectly understood language on fragments of papyrus and stone: not
voices but written words, governed by conventions very different from those
of speech. Texts may aspire to the life of 'what comes forth from the mouth',
but writing and speaking are never the same. Only when this is realised can
we hope to watch these fossilised words and catch an echo of their meaning.

   This anthology does not cover the imperial age of the New Kingdom
pharaohs but is drawn from the less spectacular world of the Middle
Kingdom, the 10th to 13th Dynasties. Though its monuments no longer
dominate the scenery of Egypt, it was a period of high culture in art and
literature which was regarded as a golden age by the later Egyptians. It is the
earliest period from which we have the evidence of a full range of written
language, which can speak to us more personally than objective archaeological artefacts. As historical evidence the texts cannot be totally trusted,
being ideologically biased, partial or propagandistic, but their subjectivity
has a vividness to capture thought. As E.M. Forster remarked of Alexandria,
'only through literature can the past be recovered' with such immediacy of
feeling.

The historical setting
Around 2130 BC the monumental record of the Old Kingdom gives way to a
'dark age' of uncertain length. Local artefacts and records are difficult to
correlate in order to provide a historical framework; their variety and poor
quality testify to the breakdown of central authority. A line of kings
continued to be buried at Memphis, but ruled from Heracleopolis. The
chronology of this 'House of Khety' (now known as the 9th and 10th
Dynasties) is uncertain, as is the extent of its rule; it has left few archaeological
remains. In the provincial capitals lines of local rulers flourished, and in the
south, at Thebes, one of these founded a dynasty of kings named Intef (the
11th Dynasty). The relationship between the various groups of powers is
unknown, but it seems that the Heracleopolitan rule over all Egypt was, at
best, very limited. The local rulers refer to battles between provinces, but by
the reign of Wahankh Intef (II), the Theban house could claim the land from
Abydos to Elephantine. Record survives of a border conflict at Abydos, which
was probably with the King Khety who features in the 'Teaching for

---

[1] Numbers in bold refer to writings translated in this anthology.

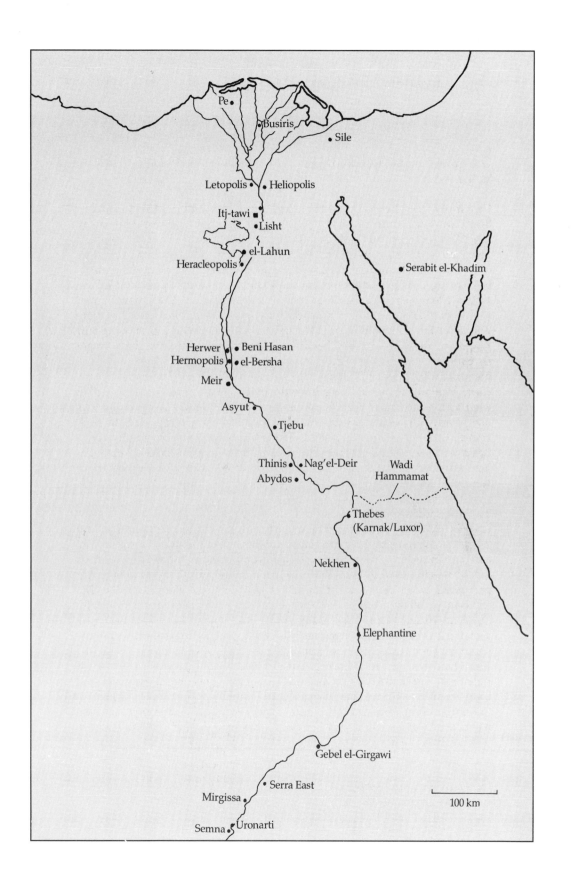

Pe •

Busiris •

• Sile

Letopolis •   • Heliopolis

Itj-tawi ◼ •
           • Lisht

           • el-Lahun

Heracleopolis •

Serabit el-Khadim •

Herwer •   • Beni Hasan
Hermopolis • • el-Bersha

Meir •

Asyut •

     • Tjebu

Thinis •   • Nag'el-Deir

Abydos •

                    Wadi
                    Hammamat

              • Thebes
                (Karnak/Luxor)

           Nekhen •

                 Elephantine •

              Gebel el-Girgawi •

           • Serra East

Mirgissa •

Semna • • Uronarti

100 km

Merikare' (**10**). Nakhtnebtepnefer Intef (III) was succeeded by Nebhetepre Montuhotep (II), who in his thirty-ninth regnal year appears as king over a unified country. The nature of this unification is, however, in doubt. None of the evidence proves that Heracleopolis fell to a military siege, and there are some indications of continuity in the administration, suggestive of a negotiated peace. The monuments of the 11th Dynasty remain concentrated in the southern part of the country.

The 12th Dynasty was founded by Amenemhat I, who had probably been the vizier of the last Montuhotep, and it was marked as the start of a new era. The capital was moved to a new site near Memphis called Itj-tawi, and administrative reforms and fortification works bore witness to a strong affirmation of the State's unity, although the process was evidently troubled. A sudden wealth of literature took the struggle against chaos as a major theme (e.g. **2, 9**). For the final ten years of the reign Prince Senwosret was adopted as coregent to ensure a peaceful succession. From the coregency there are records of military expeditions to Nubia (**31**), Libya and to the north east. His sole reign as Senwosret I, during which the consolidation of the state reached fruition, was perhaps the most important of the dynasty. It was marked by a massive building programme, honouring the royal ancestors and emulating the glory of the past. Amenemhat II ruled thirty-five years, but the chronology of the next reign, Senwosret II's, is uncertain and its length is disputed. That it was a short reign is supported by the small amount of surviving evidence for State activities such as quarrying, although Senwosret is well attested in western Asia. Such evidence represents the extent of Egypt's indirect influence rather than any empire building; an active policy continued in Nubia. The main importance of the reign for Egyptologists, however, lies in the founding of the royal funerary complex and settlement at el-Lahun (see **28**).

With Senwosret III the alternating sequence of names was broken, suggesting complications in the dynastic succession. Remains of building activity are concentrated in the south, and his most notable achievement was likewise in Nubia, with recorded campaigns in years 8, 10, 16, and 19 of his reign. The boundary was established at Semna (**6**), a further penetration into the south which was perhaps made possible by the decline of the local culture. Senwosret III was deified in Nubia and remained its patron during the New Kingdom, and echoes of his military might can be traced in the Greek historians and geographers. The royal portrait statues show the king variously, not just as idealised but also as fiercely haggard, a style which continued with great artistry under Amenemhat III. Under this king the grandiose tombs built by families of local rulers reached a peak and then ceased, and this has suggested to some that there was a major administrative reform, curbing 'feudal power'. The end of the tombs, however, may not mark the abolition of the families but a transfer of their burials to the royal cemetery; other explanations are possible. Nevertheless, these reigns seem to have marked an extensive reorganisation of the administration, and the high point of the State's centralisation. The quality of local statuary provides more concrete evidence of the regional nomarch's ability to command prestigious works. The mid-12th Dynasty was also marked by an increase in the number of private funerary chapels ('cenotaphs') in the necropolis of Abydos, which suggests a slight change in the social structure, with the rise of a limited 'sub-elite' – below the high elite, but sufficiently wealthy to afford monuments. The gradual adoption of some royal texts for private funerary ends from the end of the Old Kingdom may indicate a comparable 'democratisation' in religion, in which a wider access to the divine was permitted. At this point the dynasty's original royal cemetery of Lisht was taken over by lower-ranking officials. Nevertheless, the period was characterised by a very prescriptive vision of society, and the individual remained subservient to a rigid administration which, as indicated by the surviving documents, enforced labour duties and pursued fugitives, and had a distinctly military aspect. These features, like the division of society into a small elite and the populace, were common to all of Egyptian history; what characterises the period is the prominence of a bureaucracy in pursuit of an ideal order which was, for all its repressive qualities, explicitly founded on ethical concerns.

After Amenemhat III the house of Itj-tawi shows signs of a dynastic crisis, although the country's prosperity remained. The next king, Amenemhat IV, was probably not his predecessor's son and after a short reign was succeeded, exceptionally, by a queen, Sobekneferu, who was perhaps his wife and a daughter of Amenemhat III.

A New Kingdom king-list (the 'Turin Canon') draws a distinction between the 12th and the 13th Dynasties. Some seventy kings ruled over the next 150 years. The old royal family seems to have died out, although there was a strong sense of continuity: the capital remained at Itj-tawi and the names of several rulers echoed those of their 12th-Dynasty predecessors. The kings included a family of Sobekhoteps (though not in immediate succession). Control of lower Nubia was intially maintained and the country displayed no indications of political disintegration. The short reigns, however, are contemporaneous with a decline in the artistic products of the royal workshops. Among the families which have left most records is that of the vizier Ankhu, and there seems to have been a proliferation of all bureaucratic ranks; an increase in military titles can be seen as evidence for renewed insecurity. Except at el-Kab, the families of local rulers did not benefit from any royal weakening, and the country was apparently under the control of a centralised authority. The 13th Dynasty seems to have been a period of levelling in wealth and in general prosperity, perhaps under the influence of falling Nile levels; surviving private monuments become more numerous but can also show a sharp decline in quality, which was perhaps a direct consequence of the collapse of the royal workshops. The name of King Khendjer is symptomatic of an increasing phenomenon: it is of foreign origin, although his pyramid at Saqqara shows that he was otherwise completely Egyptianised. The infiltration of foreigners into the eastern delta culminated in a culturally distinct powerbase there, and around 1640 BC the country was divided between the 'rulers of foreign countries' (the Hyksos) in the north and a Theban state in the south. The monumental unity of the Middle Kingdom culture subsided into a dark age anathematised by later pharaohs.

Chronology

KINGS, BY DYNASTY	DATES	DOCUMENTS (probable)	DOCUMENTS (approximate)
X 'The House of Khety'	2081–1987		
Various kings called Khety, including:			1/52?
Khety Nebkaure			
Khety Merikare			55?, 57
XI Sehertawi Intef (I)	2081–2065		
Wahankh Intef (II)	2065–2016	**39a, 58?**	**39b, 39d**
Nakhtnebtepnefer Intef (III)	2016–2008		
Nebhetepre Montuhotep (II)	2008–1957		
Sankhkare Montuhotep (III)	1957–1945	**34**	
Nebtawire Montuhotep (IV)	1945–1939		**35?**
XIII 'The Kings of the Residence of Itj-tawi'			
Amenemhat I	1938–1908	**2**	**10?, 15?, 21, 23, 31, 39f-g, 56?**
Senwosret I	1918–1875	**3/51, 5, 9, 13, 16, 17, 22, 27, 31, 44, 45, 47**	
Amenemhat II	1876–1842	**14, 46?, 53**	**8?, 39h?, 50?**
Senwosret II	1844–1837	**24, 39e**	
Senwosret III	1836–1818	**6, 7, 28, 42?, 54**	
Amenemhat III	1818–1770(?)	**19, 20, 29a, 29c, 30, 32, 33, 37?**	
Amenemhat IV	1770(?)–1760(?)	**29b, 36**	**18**
Sobekneferu	1760–1756(?)		
XIII-IV 'The Kings who followed the House of Sehotepibre (Amenemhat I)'	1756(?)–1640		
Only the most important of these ephemeral kings are listed, with their approximate position in the dynasty (according to the Turin Canon):			
4 Sekhemkare Amenemhat (V)		**38c**	**12/43?, 40?, 48?, 49?**
12 Khaankhre Sobekhotep (I)			**11?**
16 Amenemhat-Sobekhotep (II)		**26**	
17 Khendjer			
21 Sekhemreswadjtawi Sobekhotep (III)			
22 Khasekhemre Neferhotep (I)			
24 Khaneferre Sobekhotep (IV)			
27 Merneferre Iy			

NB All dates given are approximate.

The nature of the writings

The script and its development

It is not just the historical context of these writings that is alien to us, living as we do in a predominantly literate culture. Writing itself meant something very different to the Egyptians from what it means to us. It is perhaps best to begin with the working of the script, which seems alarmingly complex in theory, but which is easy to read in practice. The hieroglyphic script consisted of pictorial signs, some of which conveyed phonetic information (phonograms), while others indicated meaning (semograms). Phonograms indicated a single consonant, or two or three; vowels were not recorded. The signs of meaning either represented a word pictorially (logograms), in which case they were accompanied by a stroke to indicate this (an orthogram), or were added to the end of a word to show its area of meaning (a taxogram, or determinative). These various categories complemented one another, but the combinations to be used in spelling a particular word were determined by traditional usage, rather than being a matter of bewildering choice. Thus the name Amenemhat, which means 'Amen-is-foremost', was written with a largely consistent set of signs, although sometimes the determinative – an image of a man to show that it is a man's name – was omitted:

j +	mn +	n +	m +	$ḥ3t$ +	t + stroke + determinative
(biliteral phonogram)				(logogram)	(orthogram) (taxogram)

jmn-m-$ḥ3t$

Amenemhat

Throughout Egyptian history the hieroglyphs kept their pictorial character, which made them a highly aesthetic script. They were carved or painted in varying degrees of elaboration on stone, plaster or wood, and could be written from right to left or left to right, and either vertically or horizontally. This flexibility suited their decorative function. For the sake of convenience, however, simplified forms now known as cursive hieroglyphs were soon developed, and these evolved into very abbreviated forms to be written with a pen, known as 'hieratic'. By the Middle Kingdom all three styles of script were in use, and hieratic was itself developing into two distinct types, a careful manuscript hand and a more rapid hand for administrative documents and letters. The simplified cursive hieroglyphs were drawn on walls, wood or papyrus, generally in vertical lines, while the usual writing surface for hieratic was papyrus or wooden writing boards, although graffiti can be found almost anywhere. Hieratic was always written from right to left, but both horizontally and vertically (until the end of the 13th Dynasty). These cursive scripts were the first to be learnt and very often the only ones: it is clear that many scribes had difficulties in reading the decorative hieroglyphs that are, ironically, the most familiar to us.

The most commonly used writing surface was papyrus, and as such it became the emblem of all writing things. It was made from strips cut from the marsh plant of the same name and manufactured in sheets (L. usually *c*. 40 cm and H. 30 cm) which were then joined into rolls. This process produces a durable, creamy surface which is very pleasant to write on. The side on which the strips were horizontal was used first and was the inner side of a roll (the 'recto'), while the outer (the 'verso') was composed of vertical strips which were less susceptible to cracking during rolling. Full-sized rolls were used for large-scale official documents, while literary texts tended to be written on halved rolls (H. *c*. 15 cm) or sometimes quartered rolls (H. *c*. 7.5 cm). Guidelines were often ruled to help with the laying-out of columned hieratic texts such as accounts and registers. The rolls were used over many years, with other texts, jottings, memoranda and the like being crammed into blank spaces (e.g. **26** and **33**), and with pieces even being cut out to write letters. It was commonplace to clean and reuse papyri, often several times, which suggests that they were a fairly precious commodity. Most surviving rolls were reused ('palimpsest' is the term by which such reused manuscripts are known), and new rolls were reserved for prestigious documents, such as important government records.

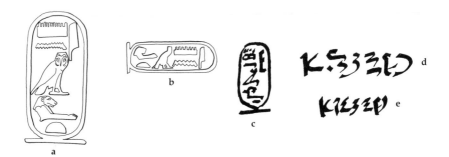

The name Amenemhat in various styles of script: (a) elaborately carved hieroglyphs, from a royal monument (BM 1072); (b) hieroglyphs carved in sunk relief, from a private stela from Abydos (Louvre C2); (c) cursive hieroglyphs, from a ritual text (P Ram. 6); (d) literary hieratic (P Ram. D: see **18**); (e) swift hieratic (Papyrus Brooklyn: see **33**). (Not to scale.)

 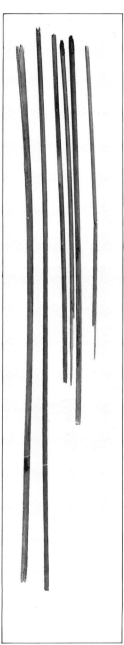

Scribal equipment (BM 5516; H. 15 cm). The palette, which was well used, has two holes for red and black ink, and a slot for reed pens. It dates from the late Middle Kingdom and was made by one Ameny for his father (whose name is lost).

The symbol of a literate man was the most characteristic equipment of a scribe: a reed pen and a palette which contained usually two cakes of ink. One was black ink, made from soot, and the other was red, from ochre. Brushes were used for painting and drawing hieroglyphs, but modern experiments suggest that the reed pens used for hieratic were actually cut, so as to produce strokes of varying thickness, although fully split reed pens are not attested until the third century BC. The pen had to be held with the hand clear of the writing surface to avoid smudging while writing from left to right. Horizontal lines were usually more swiftly written (and less legible) and fitted more words on to the papyrus; vertical lines, which used the space less economically, are more frequent in prestigious manuscripts. When we read a hieratic manuscript, we are faced with the handiwork of an all-too-human scribe. The handwriting of different scribes can still be distinguished, with each tending to make different types of error. One fault, however, is common: there is often a noticeable deterioration and hastiness towards the end of a document, as the scribe's concentration faded. A striking example of our reliance on the fallible copyist is the unique, but partially erased, copy of the 'Herdsman's Tale' (which was reused as part of the 12th-Dynasty roll containing **50**). There the hand becomes slightly swifter as the climax approaches:

> As DAY DAWNED, very early,
> it came about as he expected:
> this goddess encountered him,
> as he placed himself ‹at› the front of the pool.
> She came, naked of her clothing,
> letting her hair down

And at this point, in mid-verse, the copy breaks off, for the rest was erased, and we are left in eternal suspense.

One of the most attractive features of papyri is the use of red ink, a practical means of highlighting phrases and marking distinctions. For example, the totals in accounts were put in red, as were certain words for 'wheat' and 'emmer', to distinguish them from other grain notations. The quantities of ingredients for potions in medical and magical papyri were rubricised, as could be replies added to a letter, or insertions and corrections to a text. Perhaps the most common use of red was to indicate headings and the opening phrase of a section of a text. Thus dates were usually rubricised, although the word for 'year' remained in black, since red was also a colour of ill-omen, in which demonic names could be written, and was therefore singularly inappropriate for a king's name or regnal year. In inventories – e.g., **33** (e) – dots were used as check marks, and from these a system of punctuation was developed for literary texts. These red points marked the ends of short phrases which, as far as we can tell, correspond to lines of verse. Unfortunately they are often misplaced, and once again scribal carelessness obstructs our understanding of literary form. They appear in only one Middle Kingdom papyrus, but are widespread in the New Kingdom copies of earlier texts; while they must have aided scanning a text considerably, their late introduction shows that this was perfectly possible without them. Through-out the Middle Kingdom rubrics marked the beginnings of stanzas of verse (called 'mansions', by a metaphor similar to our modern one), but these were often omitted, particularly in vertical lines. The literary punctuation reached its maturity in the New Kingdom when it was applied more consistently; only then was a specific sign for the end of a stanza used (an abbreviation for the word 'pause': ‿ᔓ; this had occasionally marked the divisions between spells in the Middle Kingdom Coffin Texts).

The appearance of writing in Egypt, as in other cultures, is associated with the State administration: many of the earliest pieces of writing are lists and accounts. A second use was for captions on monuments, to provide the name of the owner or specify the subject represented, and this tradition of monumental display lasted throughout Egyptian history. When restricted to these functions the words did not need to be 'read' as linguistic sequences: the bare list is a fundamental genre of writing. It was only later, in the 3rd and 4th Dynasties, that continuous texts began to be written, and through the following dynasties the range of written texts expanded, although they remained centred around the original categories of display and listing. From that period we have the remains of various types of administrative documents, including decrees, letters, contracts and the like, and towards the end of the Old Kingdom the monumental record also included a large body of royal funerary spells and rituals, which presumably had been passed down until then on papyrus or orally. One particularly important formal development was the private funerary text which presented the deceased's identity, virtues and career in an 'autobiography' on the walls of his tomb or on a stela. This type of text gradually evolved from lists of the deceased's titles into sequences of formulaic epithets extolling his qualities with a narrative of his achievements. It is a measure of writing's precious rarity that it was originally restricted to the most important texts: the processes of the State, the great royal mortuary spells and the eternal epithets of the elite were the first words to be transcribed.

During the Middle Kingdom there was a sudden proliferation of written texts. Perhaps the most striking innovation was the sudden appearance of 'literature' (see pp.25–7). But where did these tales and wisdom texts come from? We assume that literature must have existed before this date in an oral form, and this assumption is supported by the fact that the sophisticated system of literary genres emerges fully formed. Despite this ancestry in the spoken word, literature showed the influence of the previous limitations of writing, especially its funerary usage. Thus wisdom literature echoed the ethical epithets and formulae of the tomb autobiographies in its didactic injunctions and gnomic reflections, and wisdom texts continued to be carved in funerary contexts (e.g., **16**). The most famous 12th-Dynasty narrative – the 'Tale of Sinuhe' **3, 51** – makes the influence of the tomb explicit by presenting itself as the protagonist's autobiography: the tomb, as a leading German Egyptologist, Jan Assmann, has remarked, was the very school of Egyptian literature. This is not in any way morbid or funereal, for the tomb was more than a place of burial. It was a symbol of the communication between the dead and the living, between eternity and human life, and this communication was a central theme of Egyptian thought and writing.

A survey of the uses of writing
The uses of writing and the role of literacy in society remained very restricted. Current estimates suggest that not more than one per cent of the population of the Middle Kingdom was literate; that is to say, about 10,000 people, a number which would have been enough to administer the country (according to better-documented parallels such as the medieval French village of Montaillou). Literacy was the preserve of the high elite, even though the practical tasks of writing were delegated to a bureaucratic sub-elite of clerks. The smallness of this writing class was not due to any inherent difficulty in learning the script, but must have reflected the fundamental cultural and economic divisions in Egyptian society. Consequently, documents can illustrate only the life and thought of this elite, and the rest of society remains an unknown continent. Literacy was, with obvious cause, extolled by the ruling class, and writing was a status symbol regardless of its content (see **27**). As such, it could hardly become a vehicle of subversive thought.

A statue of a Middle Kingdom official in the posture of a scribe (BM 2308; H. 25 cm).

Literacy has been recognised as having a powerful influence on thought processes, but in Egypt this potential was not fully realised: writing enabled the preservation and codification of information, especially ancient and esoteric information, but it did not produce any more abstract, discursive analysis of what was known, nor any cultural plurality. The only signs of these possible transformations are the phrases which were added to certain Middle Kingdom religious spells and rituals as explanatory glosses (e.g., **45** 'This is ...'). Egypt remained a largely oral culture, with writing a limited social and cognitive phenomenon.

Most often writings were probably read aloud, and they were usually introduced as transcripts of speeches, 'spoken' by the protagonist to an audience. Nevertheless, all written texts were remote from everyday speech, as can be seen in the scenes of workmen shown on tomb walls: even the words of these apparently most 'colloquial' of speakers, which are transcribed beside them, are idealised and formalised (see **22–4**). Writing was a self-sustaining system, and the written language was always distinct – almost a different tongue – from the more rapidly evolving spoken language. Common to both, however, were levels of formality with social implications. One official of Senwosret I, the steward Montuwoser, declares on his funerary stela:

> 'I was one who spoke according to the language of the officials, one free from saying *p3*s.'

p3 is equivalent to the English 'the' or 'this' and it was then considered too colloquial both for the formal language of court circles and for texts. Elements of everyday speech such as this permeated the writings very slowly, and their progress reveals a hierarchy of written style. The phase of the written language in which *p3* occurs is now termed 'late Middle Egyptian', and is first found in practical documents, such as letters and accounts (e.g., **28–30**): these are the most colloquial texts. This happens in the early Middle Kingdom; by the 12th–13th Dynasties elements of late Middle Egyptian appeared in some of the less elaborate literary texts (particularly fictional narratives such as **11**). The formal written language of the 12th Dynasty – classical Middle Egyptian – was still used for monumental and religious texts, but by the 18th Dynasty features of late Middle Egyptian had permeated even royal inscriptions. At this date late Middle Egyptian was probably already further removed from everyday speech than Middle Egyptian had been in the 12th; only after the 18th Dynasty was it considered suitable for religious and funerary texts. A comparable hierarchy existed in the use of the various scripts. Thus practical documents (including collections of technical knowledge) and letters were written in a rapid form of hieratic, while a more elegant form tended to be used for high literature. Cursive hieroglyphs were reserved for religious and ritual texts (e.g., **1, 45, 52**), and neat copies of technical texts, as is shown by a veterinary papyrus from an el-Lahun library, perhaps because they were an archaic-looking hand suitable for ancient wisdom. The decorative, fully drawn hieroglyphs were used for private and State monuments, which were largely religious or funerary. As most scribes were involved primarily with

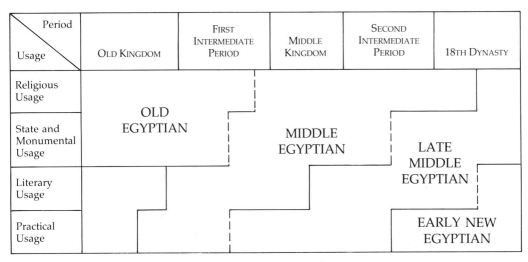

A table of language and texts (after Junge, LÄ V, 1176–1211, table 2).

everyday administration, hieratic and the cursive script were the basis of scribal training, together with the stylistically equivalent phase of the language. As noted above, a literate person's reading ability of the monumental forms was often fairly limited; a later example of this limitation can be found in **59b**.

A related question is the rather controversial one of 'verse', or rather of metre: can Egyptian 'prose' and 'verse' be distinguished? The most widely accepted theory is that pioneered by Gerhard Fecht, who argues that 'verse' existed and was composed in accentuated 'lines' based on the stress patterns of the language. In this interpretation, metre tightly patterns most texts, except for those where the pattern is created by other means, such as the physical arrangement of accounts in columns on the page. Similarly, the decorative hieroglyphs on monuments, which are emblematic and not to be read linguistically, are apparently not in metre. Purely practical documents are problematic in relation to metre: some decrees and letters to the dead are written in formal verse, but others show no strict metrical pattern when accentuated (see p.30). It seems that such texts, in which the immediate conveying of information naturally took precedence over considerations of form, lay close to, or beyond, the boundaries of metre. As so often in Egyptology, more research is required before the question can be settled with any finality.

The subject matter of texts was also governed by a strict decorum which determined what could be included in various types of text. This was not the result of State censorship but a self-perpetuating tradition, such as can be found in most literature, where certain themes are considered appropriate for certain genres. The royal monumental record, for instance, contained an ideological pageant of ritualised history, from which individual irregularities were excluded, and the same concern with eternal order runs through non-royal tomb inscriptions. There is never a mention of adultery in these, but in wisdom texts it is alluded to as a danger (e.g., **15** maxims 18, 21) and in private letters it is a bluntly stated concern (e.g., **34b**). In a 20th-Dynasty letter to the Theban scribe Tjaroy there is a striking example of this inevitable dichotomy between the decorous presentation of events according to ideology and what actually went on: here the supposedly all-powerful pharaoh is scornfully dismissed by a military leader – a royal deputy:

> 'I've listened to all the matters about which you sent to me. As for this matter you mentioned – these two Medjai, saying "they told about these matters" – join with Nodjme, and Payshuuben as well, and they'll send and have these two Medjai brought to this House and they'll get to the bottom of their words – very thoroughly! – until they can speak truly! You shall put them in two baskets and throw them into the river at night – but don't let anyone in this land know! Another matter: As for Pharaoh l.p.h., how shall he reach this land? Now, as for Pharaoh l.p.h., whose superior (is he) in any case?'

This private message betrays the growing political disintegration within the elite of that period, which was not represented directly in the monumental record.

The texts carved on State monuments formulated the established view of the universe without qualification, but wisdom texts and tales explored the dark side of life much more freely. One example will suffice: in the fictional autobiography of Sinuhe (**3**) the Egyptian experience of life is profoundly questioned through his exile, whereas this dilemma between Egyptian and other values is never envisaged in actual tomb autobiographies. Nevertheless all potentially tragic elements are given some sort of harmonious resolution. No texts were handed down which directly subverted the mainstream tradition of ideas and values: Sinuhe always returned to Egypt in the end.

Various hierarchies and systems of decorum ordered the various types of writings, but how can these be individually characterised? How can the whole body of writings be categorised? It is difficult to do this because there is no distinct Egyptian terminology to help us, and this absence is part of a more general lack of analytical vocabulary. Many of the terms applied to texts simply describe their practical purpose (such as *wd*, a 'command'), while the blanket term 'writings' is used of a wide range of documents. Certain general terms had a specialised usage, such as 'teaching' (*sb3jjt*), which could mean anything didactic or could denote a strictly defined literary form. The definition of genres, and of 'literature' itself, is problematic in any written culture, and is especially difficult when the culture lies outside the familiar Western tradition. In the next few pages I survey the different types of text according to their forms, contents and contexts. I group them into practical texts of information, technical texts, religious and magical texts, tomb texts, commemorative texts and the great tradition of literature.

Many texts can be defined by their obvious, pragmatic purpose – to communicate and record information. These most probably formed the major part of what was written, but only an imbalanced and minuscule selection of this writing survives (see pp.28–9). Sets of accounts (27) can easily be recognised by their arrangement in columns, and their phrasing has little to do with spoken words: 2 gallons of grain is expressed in tabulated form as 'grain: 2 gallons'. The influence of this listing convention on other types of text is seen in the 19th-Dynasty 'Tale of The Two Brothers' when a handsome muscular cowherd who is carrying fodder is admiringly asked: 'How much do you have on your shoulders?' This looks like a transcription of speech, but his reply is written down as 'Emmer: 3 sacks; barley: 2 sacks; total 5'! More extensive records are found in institutional daybooks (27–8), in which events as well as expenditures were listed. Annals and king-lists applied the same principle to the history of the State, which was articulated as a sequence of kings (cf. 8) and, more fully, as a list of regnal years with notes describing the principal event(s) of each year. Similarly, the surviving examples of legal registers are often expanded lists, which make use of accounting-style abbreviations (33), and a similar approach is found in contracts and court proceedings (36–8). Decrees (26) and letters (28–30, 34–5, 55–7) show the same tendencies (e.g., the use of 'Also: …' in 34). Written formalism is also demonstrated by the presence of tightly structured verse in some of these, most obviously in those decrees which were copied on to monuments for permanence and publicity, and in letters addressed to the dead. The monumental durability of these communications may have encouraged a greater awareness of form. All of this forces us to realise how remote such texts are from being simple voices from the past.

Technical texts existed, which provided catalogues itemising practical knowledge of mathematics and medicine. They are not treatises but lists of particular empirical problems and solutions, which were intended to act as general models (19–20). Their characteristic structure is exemplified in the so-called 'onomastica' (18), which are epitomes of the Egyptian tradition of knowledge as compendia of terminology. To know a word or a name was to understand the subject, an attitude which pervaded magic and religion, where power was provided by the knowledge of names and rituals were structured by word-play (e.g., 45). The modern reader who does not readily consider these texts to be 'literature' should perhaps think again. The early 18th-Dynasty medical manuscript known as Papyrus Ebers, for example, shows no signs of wear (unlike 20), which suggests that it was kept for purposes other than practical use, namely as a source of knowledge for its own sake. Many surviving rolls are not from temple libraries but from tombs, where they were buried beside their owners. This grouping of technical texts with high literary texts in one Middle Kingdom private library implies that the Egyptian conception of literature was broader than our own, and similar to the older European belles-lettres which also included scientific treatises. From this Egyptian literature can be defined as a body of written high culture with purposes other than the merely necessary communication of practical information. Within this literature there was a significant body of texts which were more concerned with aesthetically structured form and were consistently composed in verse: religious, funerary and monumental texts. There was also a smaller group of texts in which aesthetic considerations were primary. This latter group corresponds to the popular modern idea of things 'literary', and I will use the term to describe this group alone.

Religion provided occasions for writing as well as administration. Among texts from the temples we find copies of rituals, used for reference and in performance, including funerary rituals, as well as the procedures and recitations for the daily cult and regular festivals (**45**). Hymns were especially important in ceremonies, but were also a vehicle for religious knowledge and doctrine (**7, 41**). They can display considerable literary artifice, and aesthetic form is often the key to their structure. Magic existed side by side with other forms of knowledge and collections of spells were arranged like technical texts, except that they were stylistically different because they were more concerned with incantation than with action or calculation (**49**). Narrative myths are attested, but they apparently did not have a major role in the written tradition of religion, and hymns fulfilled the descriptive function which myths often have elsewhere. Myths may well have played a more prominent part in oral culture (see **42**). The walls of temples provided a vast potential for writing, beyond the libraries of papyri contained within those buildings. The walls were decorated with tableaux portraying episodes from the daily cult, accompanied by captions describing the actions and recording the relevant words, as well as by more emblematic hieroglyphs which were parts of the representational iconography (see **44**). These illustrative captions are very repetitive and rarely long, but one example which may derive from the Middle Kingdom is extremely, and almost uniquely, discursive about doctrinal matters (**4**).

Closely related to the religious writings were the funerary spells, which are the most extensive single body of surviving texts, not only because of their cultural importance, but also because the chances of preservation always favour tombs (**1, 52**). These did not form a canon of sacred scriptures, and they display local variations incompatible with such a system. They related primarily to magic and ritual practices, and were used by both the living and the dead. Although they were 'utterances' to be recited, there was a strong sense of them as written documents, probably because writing and esoteric wisdom were viewed as closely related phenomena: thus the most powerful spells were called 'that which is upon the end of the roll' (**1**). Like the hymns and technical texts, the spells alluded to knowledge without direct exposition or exegesis, although some have a strong expository character, such as those which describe the Netherworld – almost incantatory guidebooks (e.g., **52**).

The dead had other texts than these: those from funerary monuments and grave goods. Many were simply labels giving the tomb-owner's titles, but there were also captions to the scenes of life decorating tomb walls and stelae (see **21–4, 39, 48**). These included scenes of funerary rituals with the relevant words, including harpist's songs (**47, 58**). One song (**58**) has been preserved in a 19th-Dynasty collection of love-lyrics, whose scribe obviously valued its musical and aesthetic character as well as its role in ceremonial 'beatifications'. Of all tomb texts the most distinctive and influential genre was the autobiography, which consisted of the owner's titles followed by a self-eulogy. These elaborate compositions had a practical aim of communicating the virtue of the dead to the living, as an inspiration to maintain the funerary cult. They appeal to the living to recite the funerary formula which invokes an 'offering-which-the-king-gives' for the deceased, a formula that is repeated on walls, stelae and grave goods throughout the tomb (**13, 40, 53–4**). The eulogy is a genre which occurs elsewhere in hymns and royal inscriptions. All these written forms share the same oral antecedent of the praise song. Self-eulogies were not limited to the dead, but could also be attributed to gods in ritual and funerary texts (**1**) and to kings. In funerary autobiographies the deceased acclaimed his life as ethically ideal, a theme which was also central to wisdom literature. The historical and thematic relationship between these two types of text (see pp.17–18) was still acknowledged in the 12th Dynasty, when the Patrician and Count Sehotepibre carved an edited version of the 'Loyalist Teaching' (**16**) on his stela. The autobiographies often contained a narrative section in which perfect conduct was exemplified more specifically and historically, and this also had considerable influence on other written genres.

Funerary inscriptions have been termed 'monumental', as if this were a particular genre of texts. Other 'monumental' texts include the illustrative captions in temples, but there is every reason to suppose that similar texts existed in secular buildings, indeed on any surface used for representation, regardless of its 'monumentality'. Papyri, furniture, amulets, wine-jars and seals demonstrate the common use of writing for labelling objects and expressing ownership. Many 'monumental' texts are enlarged examples of this type: rock inscriptions labelled the level of a high Nile level or named a canal and commemorated its digging. Other examples show the same derivation from non-monumental models: decrees and temple rituals are made monumental for durability and display. In most cases 'monumental' is a category which is defined by the writing surface used for the text and not by the genre of the text itself, although only certain genres and styles were deemed suitable for a monument. For example, the Semna stela (**6**) is essentially a royal order copied on to stone as a boundary marker, although it is a suitably formal and grandiose example of the genre. However, there was a type of text which was by definition exclusively monumental: the commemorative inscription. The graffiti made by members of desert expeditions were in many cases modelled on funerary stelae and auto-biographies (e.g., **31**), or on other types of text (e.g., **8**, which recalls annalistic king-lists), but they also show a tendency towards monumental commemoration for its own sake. And this was fully expressed in the inscriptions recording mining expeditions to the Eastern Desert and Sinai (e.g., **32**). The monumental style of inscription was used by Middle Kingdom royalty, although it rose to greater prominence in the New Kingdom. The early royal examples betray the same models as the private ones; in particular, those dealing with historical events seem to have developed directly from private autobiographies, although they also show the influence of fictional narratives (**5**). A common stylistic feature reveals another ancestor: the narrative progresses through a sequence of infinitives ('The king's going south. The king's ordering …'), such as are found in the brief headings and captions in annals and daybooks.

The group of texts which corresponds to the narrow concept of high literature is preserved to a limited extent in privately owned copies from the Middle Kingdom. Another more plentiful source comes from the New Kingdom, when they were organised into a corpus of 'set texts' for teaching scribes the then 'classical' language of Middle Egyptian. Their appeal lay not just in their language, but also in their status as established classics (**60**). This cohesive and distinct group contains wisdom texts and fictional narratives. They are stylistically very complex (although some late Middle Kingdom narratives become less elaborate), and all are reasonably short: even the comparatively lengthy 'Tale of the Eloquent Peasant' is only some 630 verse-lines long. With few exceptions, these literary compositions were identified in terms of their protagonists, not their authors: most of Egyptian literature is anonymous. Only wisdom texts had titles, which described them as spoken by a particular individual, perhaps because wisdom is essentially a personal quality. The texts were often attributed to sages who were already long dead at the date of composition (probably because the truest wisdom is the most ancient), and these sages were later eulogised as if they were the authors (**60a**). Yet it is clear from the same source (**60b**) that at least one of the wisdom texts was recognised as pseudonymous; its praise of the scribe Khety shows that the concept of an individual author who was famed for his fine compositions could exist, although it was not central to the literary tradition. Khety is probably the only Middle Kingdom author known to us by name.

Wisdom texts were 'perfect speech' (**15**), which meant not just fine rhetoric, but 'spoken perfection'. They were the articulation of perfection and Truth, and Ptahhotep could say of his maxims: 'As for their Truthfulness, this is their value' (l. 509; see **15**). Their Truth was ethical, abstract and eternal, yet its perfection had also an aesthetic aspect: Truth was beauty, and fine style was the inevitable correlative of high ethics. Thus instructive words were also intended to entertain and give pleasure. Even the grimly apocalyptic 'Prophecy of Neferti' (**2**) is spoken in response to a royal request to:

> 'Speak to me a few perfect words,
>
> choice verses, whose hearing will give my Person enjoyment.'

Two principal types of wisdom literature can be identified. One is the 'Teaching' genre, which took the form of a didactic statement made by a father to his child(ren) on the nature of the ideal life. The protagonists included specific royal and official personages (e.g., **9, 10, 15–17**), who were often located in a past golden age, although one example is more universal and is spoken simply 'by a man to his son'. The context of a father passing on wisdom often led to a narrative framework, but the Teachings, although supposedly composed for a particular occasion, were always concerned with eternal values (**15**). The second group includes more reflective texts which are characterised by gnomic epigrams, and which arise from more problematic fictional contexts than the 'Teachings'. They comprised two distinct genres, the 'Lament', describing Truth through its absence in a chaotic world (**2, 12,**

43), and the 'Discourses', which were more general meditations on similar themes (**14**). The discursive character of these texts meant that many were conceived as dialogues (e.g., **50** and **12/43**).

The last literary genre to be listed, which made a late appearance in the written record, is the most easily appreciated by us: the fictional narrative (**3, 11, 51**). It must hark back to oral antecedents, although most Middle Kingdom examples display elaboration of a type completely incompatible with a direct 'folk' origin. The 'Tale of Sinuhe' (**3/51**), for example, includes a dazzling variety of literary forms, many of them specifically written forms, while the plain style of tales such as 'The Shipwrecked Sailor' is a mock simplicity, disguising a complex treatment of high moral and religious themes. Both of these tales are told by the hero, and the frequency of this use of the first person narrator may reflect the influence of the tomb autobiographies, the earliest formal texts with narrative elements. Tales told in the third person are equally sophisticated, although from the late 12th Dynasty on they showed more features characteristic of folk tales and were written in more colloquial language. This is not due to a popularisation of high literature, but probably can be explained as the start of the broadening of literary decorum, which produced a marked stylistic difference between the literature of the Middle and New Kingdoms.

The total number of written texts was small by modern standards. The small size of the corpus accounts for the remarkable degree of cross-fertilisation which is found between various literary and non-literary types. Symptoms of this close intertextuality are the wide range of genres which drew on the same common formulaic expressions, and the mingling of genres. Different ones were combined in single literary works, such as the 'Tale of the Eloquent Peasant' (**14**), which is both a tale and a series of discourses with elements of 'Teachings' and 'Laments'. This fluidity is a measure of how different Egyptian literature was from the more rigid classical tradition, which has shaped Western literature; another indication is the minor role of the author. Even with 'The Teaching of Amenemhat' (**9**), which was acknowledged as the work of Khety, there was no mention of the author in the title. There was no sense of a literary work having a single authorised form, and different copies can show great textual variations. As a text was transmitted it mutated – lines were adapted, added or deleted – so that not only is it difficult to reconstruct an original text from the surviving manuscripts, but it can also be doubtful whether the text we have was composed by any single individual. This may reflect the largely oral context – oral compositions are not restricted by any single recorded version. Nevertheless, the high literature was presented as specifically written, and *correctly* written! Literary manuscripts concluded with a colophon which referred to the work as part of high culture needing accurate transmission: 'IT IS COME FROM BEGINNING TO END, AS FOUND IN WRITING.' At the end of the manuscript of the 'Tale of the Shipwrecked Sailor' the copyist made a rather smug addition: 'AS WRITTEN BY THE SCRIBE, EXCELLENT OF FINGERS, AMENY'S SON AMENYAA L.P.H.' As this is the only known copy of the tale, we can have no idea how true this claim is.

In conclusion, there are two noticeable omissions in this description of Middle Kingdom literature: dramatic writings and secular lyrics. No drama, as the West knows it, survives from any period of Egyptian history, although there are rituals designed for a performance which would re-enact a myth through symbols and dialogue (e.g., **45**). Performance was also an important aspect of literature; texts other than hymns and eulogies would have been 'recited' or 'sung', and the high literature was probably often recited before an audience, as well as being read privately. This performative element should not be underestimated: tomb autobiographies are the self-eulogies of dead men and as such might be thought singularly inappropriate for a performative reading. Nevertheless, one stela indicates that they were read aloud by scribes to the non-literate (quoted in the introduction to **53**). More remarkably, in the tomb of the 10th-Dynasty nomarch Khety II at Asyut, one of the inscriptions addresses the deceased in the second person: there is no standard autobiographical 'I was ...', only 'You were ...'. Although the passage is fragmentary and the context problematic, this suggests that the autobiographies could be oral performances addressed to the deceased, as well as written memorials for the passer-by to read. This fragment betrays our ignorance of the spoken word, and of the relationship between oral and written forms.

Our ignorance is also shown by the lack of lyric songs from the Middle Kingdom. There are examples of harpist's songs (**21, 47, 58**), which are clearly ritual in character, but copies of secular love songs do not appear before the 19th Dynasty. It is hard to imagine that such lyrics did not exist earlier; rather, they probably lay outside what was considered suitable for writing. Support for this is found in examples of written song from the tomb of the nomarch Count Djehutihotep at el-Bersha (see **24, 39**). In one scene men are shown dragging a colossal statue of him to his funerary complex. The men's 'recitation' is recorded beside them:

> 'Beloved of Thoth is Djehutihotep, the beloved of the king,
> loved by his town, favoured by all its gods;
> the temples are in festival, their hearts joyful,
> seeing your favours from the king!'

On the lap of the statue stands a cheer-leader who 'gives the beat' to them, with the refrain:

> 'Djehutihotep, beloved of the king!'

This work-song is no doubt formalised and idealised like the workmen's speeches from other tomb walls (e.g., **22–4**), and it will not be exactly what the workers sang on the rocky road to el-Bersha 3,800 years ago; but it is certain demonstration that such songs, which are still common in Egypt today, did exist even though they usually went unrecorded. It is an indication of the oral world that is completely lost to us. That world's passing would perhaps not have distressed the elite: literacy and writing were not only the vehicles by which their high culture was transmitted; they ranked among the very symbols of its primacy.

The nature of the anthology

'To seek among phrases and fragments something unbroken.'
(Virginia Woolf, *The Waves*)

This anthology has two aims. One is to provide a representative sample of every type of written text, rather than just a narrow selection of Egyptian literature, which is readily available elsewhere. The other is to use the writings to illustrate life in the Middle Kingdom. The texts are arranged by subject into six sections, and grouped within these into culturally self-aware statements and more practical, everyday documents. This distinction avoids the 'documentary' fallacy of treating literary texts merely as sources of historical evidence rather than as works of art. The 'Teaching for Merikare' (**10**) is an example of the dangers of this fallacy: it has been repeatedly analysed for historical information about the 10th Dynasty, regardless of its essentially ahistorical nature. However one defines literature, it is a complex form of discourse which resists such reductionist analysis. This distinction between literary and practical texts would have appealed to the writers of the Middle Kingdom, through whose compositions runs an awareness of the difference between the ideal and the actual.

A final, and rather more personal, consideration in choosing the texts has been a sense of freshness and fun; thus I have included no more than a representational sample of texts such as accounts, whose appeal is rather limited.

The material for the anthology is restricted in two ways. The usefulness of the texts as illustrations of Middle Kingdom life is influenced by the decorum with which they treat their subject-matter. Some important aspects of Egyptian culture were also central to its self-presentation: the king, in particular, was a vehicle for cultural definition and in consequence dominated the written sources, acting out the nation's history with various formulae. Other equally central aspects, however, were not recorded, simply because they were self-evident to the audience: there was no need to write them down. Egyptologists have argued in numerous discussions that the concept of *Maat* ('Truth' and 'Order') was the basis of Eyptian thought, yet it was never elucidated by the Egyptians themselves. This is partly a result of their general lack of any explicit analysis but it is also due to Maat's all-importance: why describe what everyone in the elite knew? Only occasionally were such widely held ideas discussed in writing, and the cases where this happened have a unique importance for us, even though they are rather unrepresentative in their choice of subject-matter (e.g., **1, 4**). They make explicit what is implicit throughout other texts. While these concepts were rarely focused upon, on the other hand some knowledge was so esoteric that it could not be written down, and was only alluded to.

Time has imposed the most insurmountable restriction on the anthology. The language is over 1,000 years dead and it is difficult even to provide a basic translation. Another problem is preservation, since most of what was written has been lost. The number of perfectly preserved texts is as alarmingly small as the number of perfectly understood ones, and an anthology has to include fragments and problematic texts. This means that there are many restorations, which are often very tentative, and unknown words, which are either left untranslated or guessed at. But the reader who is distracted by the indications of such lacunae should remember that the originals themselves cannot be read easily. An anthology of clear and complete documents would be deceptive. More generally, the range of the surviving writings is also unbalanced. Few settlement sites have preserved any sizeable archives and thus administrative documents are bound to be under-represented; most of the Middle Kingdom examples are from a single site, the pyramid town of el-Lahun. This crucial find consists of documents from at least three different archives: one belonging to a temple library and administrative records (**7, 20, 28**), another belonging to an official called Horemsaf (**29a, 29c**), and another from a more general administrative collection (**29b, 29d, 36, 37, 38**). The groups of papyri found in tombs are more numerous, and of these, two collections were deliberately deposited as libraries for the deceased. The larger one, of twenty-three rolls, was built up over almost a century and was placed in a lector priest's tomb which was eventually overlaid by the funerary temple of Ramses II (the so-called 'Ramesseum Papyri': **3/51, 14, 18, 30, 45**). The other library contained the four literary papyri acquired by Giovanni Athanasi some time before 1843 which are now in Berlin (the 'Berlin library': **3/51, 14, 50**). They must have come from a private 12th-Dynasty burial, and although the name of their owner will never be known, his taste is deservedly famous: each of them is a masterpiece. These libraries accompanied their owners to be read in eternity, as did other individual rolls, such as Papyrus Prisse (**15**). Some major tomb finds, however, were more accidental collections: the choice of rolls placed in a scribe's tomb at Nag' el-Deir seems to have been made randomly (see **27**), and the Heqanakht papers (**34**) were simply swept into a burial as debris.

All the well-preserved texts come from funerary sites on the desert edge; all the manuscripts of settlements in the valley have rotted away under modern cultivation. It is the Egyptians' concern with death which has assured the survival of their writings, and it is not surprising that much of what we have concerns the dead. A number of letters addressed to the dead (see **55–7**) have survived, posted in tombs. Letters to the living must have far outnumbered them in daily life, but those to the dead are not only better preserved, but also peculiarly accessible to us: they were written to be read across the boundary of death, even as we read them. The chasm between the original sender and recipient ensured an explicit expression of subject-matter, which is generally only alluded to in correspondence between living acquaintances. The awareness of man's impermanence has given these personal documents a rare transparency.

These restrictions and limitations remind us that it is all but impossible to recall the past. The dead cannot simply speak to us, and a voice, like love, cannot be traced in the archaeological record. Even the most personal of the letters to the dead is merely a distant reflection of the writer's voice and thoughts, in a lost language. Nevertheless, these broken texts are all that we can hope to have: 'A few verses of poetry is all that survives of David and Jonathan.' And perhaps that is enough.

Technical note

Inevitably, my translations rely heavily on the works acknowledged in the references, although no specific debts are mentioned. The fluent versions of Miriam Lichtheim provide a shining example for the translator, but I have preferred to retain some less-than-fluent literalness in order to give a flavour of the ancient idioms. I have also been freer in indicating doubtful points, lacunae and the like.

The following conventions are used:

(...)	a phrase inserted for clarification in translation.
‹...›	a phrase omitted in error by the scribe.
{...}	a phrase included in error by the scribe.
[...]	a lacuna, whose length is suggested by the number of dots. Restorations are given wherever possible, even when only the sense and not the exact words can be guessed. Particularly dubious guesses are marked (?).
CAPITALS	correspond to red ink in the original. An exception is where a rubric marks the start of a verse stanza; this is indicated with the modern convention. Numbers in red ink in the original are in bold type.
italics	are used for words whose meaning is unknown, which are transliterated into a pronounceable form.
'...'	enclose only those phrases which are explicitly designated as speech.
1	bold numbers refer to the number of a text translated in this anthology.

I have followed the metrical principles pioneered by Gerhard Fecht, with slight variation in his rules, in that I am more ready to recognise a few one-colon and four-cola verses. I have relied on manuscripts with rubrics for separating the verses into stanzas, and have used these as models for the texts without such markings. However, as explained on p.20, I have not applied his system to all texts. One obvious exception is in accounts, where the main structuring device is the arrangement into columns and registers on the page; this is retained in the translations. The applicability of metre to letters and memoranda has been doubted, and I have found in preparing these texts that they do not reveal the same tightly meaningful patterns when metricised. Consequently I have rendered these categories into English prose, despite much hesitation, and the realisation that this may not be an exactly equivalent form.

It remains to add that my interpretations of the texts and their world remain, inevitably, personal: the Egypt I have tried to recall shows the influence of the liberal humanist tradition, and my treatment of the texts that of hermeneutic criticism.

The writings

The intellectual setting of cosmos and State

The Egyptians perceived the universe in terms of a dualism between *Maat* – 'Truth' and 'Order' – and disorder. The creator god summoned the cosmos out of undifferentiated chaos by distinguishing the two, by giving voice to the ultimate ideal of Truth, which was, in mythological terms, his daughter. Despite his creative word, there remained a tendency towards disorder and decay throughout the cosmos and in the hearts of his creations. To uphold Truth both the gods and men had to struggle against this tendency. On a cosmic level it was manifest in the solar cycle, in which the creator god had repeatedly to vanquish the forces of darkness. On an earthly level the king imposed order on men, enacting the god's control in political terms, within the limitations of humanity. His single rule had to restrain the destructive and predatory impulses in society. The forces of chaos were multitudinous and disordered, while the ideal Truth was a single harmonious entity, running through the cosmos and society, and included the concept of reciprocity and retribution by which 'all that happens is bound together' (**10**).

Man's realisation of Truth was often partial. Much Middle Kingdom thinking was concerned with the difference between the ideal, as realised by the divine, and man's attempts to embody this on earth (see **14**). The constant theme of the wisdom literature was the 'acting out' of Truth on earth. This dichotomy was formulated in a historicising myth in which the order at creation was ideal, until men rebelled against the god's ordinance (a concept alluded to in **1**). It was thus the will of man that perpetrated the imperfection of the world and released chaos into it. God's response was to punish mankind with partial destruction, and to distance himself from this impurity (**2**; compare **10**). In human history the cosmic forces of chaos were revealed in social terms and described in nightmarish visions of political disorder and collapse (**2**). History would fluctuate between order and disorder, from generation to generation, and eventually end in a return to primordial chaos, in which only the creator would survive (see **1**).

These analyses were the products of a small group of the elite, and we have no way of knowing how widely they were disseminated among the populace. They were also ethnocentric: 'living according to Truth' was the Egyptian way of life, while the surrounding nomadic nations were peripheral, tending more closely towards chaos. Although the State might at times realise Truth imperfectly, and that ideal existed beyond society, Truth and the Egyptian State were inherently linked. The importance of the State is clearly felt in the 'Tale of Sinuhe' (**3**).

31

Coffin Text spell 1130 is written in cursive hieroglyphs on the floor of the inner coffin of the Chief Physician Gewa, from el-Bersha (BM 30840; H. 22 cm). He was a subordinate of the nomarch Djehutihotep (see **24, 39e**).

1 The order of the creator: Coffin Text Spell 1130

The Coffin Texts were a body of spells to ensure survival in the next world, so called from their being written principally on early Middle Kingdom coffins in cursive hieroglyphs. They are first attested at the end of the Old Kingdom, but are characteristic of Middle Kingdom burials. Even after the reunification they remained uncodified, full of variations and local traditions.

This spell is the conclusion of a series about the passage through the Netherworld, the so-called 'Book of the Two Ways', and is unique in including a declaration made by the creator god during his cosmic voyage across the sky as the sun. In this he asserts that the order which he created was just and perfect until flawed by man's deeds, and proclaims his supremacy as originator and maintainer of the world. This ideal order, although described in a cosmic setting, is very much concerned with social justice, and with giving men no cause to prey upon each other. Then the dead man speaks a series of grandiose claims and epithets, through which he assimilates himself with the power of the creator, and becomes invincible and unrestrainable in the Netherworld. This section is distinguished from the first by a change to red ink. These repetitive and incantatory utterances allude to esoteric religious knowledge which is nowhere recorded explicitly, and as such they are typical of the spells as a whole. Through both halves of the text runs the idea of imposing an ideal ethical order on chaos, which is represented by images of storm and serpents, as well as by mankind's tendency to evil.

At the end of the spell is a description of its effect; this was usually written in red, but as red was already being used, the scribe changed to black to mark it as separate.

> WORDS SPOKEN BY HIM WHOSE NAMES ARE HIDDEN.
> The Lord to the Limit speaks
> before those who still the storm, at the sailing of the entourage:
>
> 'Proceed in peace!
> I shall repeat to you four good deeds
> that my own heart made for me
> within the serpent's coils, for love of stilling evil.
> I did four good deeds within the portals of the horizon:

I made the four winds that every man might breathe in his
    place.
This is one deed thereof.
I made the great inundation, that the wretched should have
    power over it like the great.
This is one deed thereof.
I made every man like his fellow;
I did not ordain them to do evil, (but) it was their own hearts
    which destroyed that which I pronounced.[1]
This one deed thereof.
I made that their hearts should refrain from ignoring the west,
for love of making offerings to the gods of the nomes.
This is one deed thereof.
I created the gods from my sweat.
Man is from the tears of my eye.[2]

I shine, and am seen every day
in this authority of the Lord to the Limit.
I made the night for the Weary-hearted.[3]
I will sail aright in my bark;
I am the lord of the waters, crossing heaven.
I do not suffer for any of my limbs.
Utterance together with Magic[4]
are felling for me that evil being.
I shall see the horizon and dwell within it.
I shall judge the wretch from the powerful,
and do likewise against the evildoers.
Life is mine; I am its lord.
The sceptre shall not be taken from my hand.
I have placed millions of years
between me and that Weary-hearted one, the son of Geb;
then I shall dwell with him in one place.
Mounds will be towns.
Towns will be mounds.
Mansion will destroy mansion.'[5]

---

[1] The pronouncement of the Creator is 'Truth'.

[2] A word play between 'man' (*rmt*) and 'tears' (*rmjjt*) which evokes the tearfulness of the human condition.

[3] The Weary-hearted one is Osiris, the god of the dead. He and the creator, the 'lord of life' are the two poles of divinity.

[4] Two personifications of the god's creative power, who combat the personification of chaos ('that evil being').

[5] The life of the created world is alluded to as the period the creator god, the lord of life, spends apart from Osiris, the son of the earth god, Geb. At the end of the world the two gods will reunite.

I AM THE LORD OF FIRE WHO LIVES ON TRUTH,
THE LORD OF ETERNITY, MAKER OF JOY, AGAINST WHOM THE
  OTHERWORLDLY SERPENTS HAVE NOT REBELLED.
I AM THE GOD IN HIS SHRINE, THE LORD OF SLAUGHTER, WHO CALMS
  THE STORM,
WHO DRIVES OFF THE SERPENTS, THE MANY-NAMED WHO COMES
  FORTH FROM HIS SHRINE,
THE LORD OF WINDS WHO FORETELLS THE NORTHWIND,
MANY-NAMED IN THE MOUTH OF THE ENNEAD,
LORD OF THE HORIZON, CREATOR OF LIGHT,
WHO ILLUMINES HEAVEN WITH HIS OWN BEAUTY.
I AM HE! MAKE WAY FOR ME
SO THAT I SHALL SEE NIU AND AMEN.[6]
FOR I AM A BLESSED SPIRIT, EQUIPPED WITH OTHERWORLDLY
  KNOWLEDGE;
I SHALL PASS BY THE FEARFUL ONES —
‹THEY CANNOT SPEAK (THE SPELL)› WHICH IS ON THE END OF THE
  BOOK-ROLL;
THEY CANNOT SPEAK FOR FEAR OF HIM WHOSE NAME IS CONCEALED,
  WHO IS WITHIN MY BODY.
I KNOW HIM; I AM NOT IGNORANT OF HIM.
I AM EQUIPPED, EXCELLENT IN OPENING PORTALS.

As for any man who knows this spell,
he shall be like Re in the east of heaven,
like Osiris within the Netherworld;
he descends into the entourage of fire,
without there being a flame being against him, for all time and
  eternity!

2 A vision of chaos: from the 'Prophecy of Neferti'

The 'Prophecy of Neferti' is a literary discourse preserved in twenty-two New Kingdom copies, but which was, from internal evidence, composed in the early years of the 12th Dynasty. The modern title derives from the introductory narrative in which the sage Neferti amuses the good King Sneferu (2575–2551BC) with a prophecy of 'what is to come'. His speech unfolds a vision of social and cosmic chaos invading the land, which is eventually driven out by the arrival of a king who restores order. This king's name alludes to the founder of the 12th Dynasty.

The excerpt is characteristic of the 'lament' genre, and describes disorder in Egypt with images of reversal and decline. It is essentially ahistorical, and articulates an awareness of the darker side of the world, of the ever-present threats to, and imperfections in, the order. Although the 'chaos' evoked here is social, it leads to a disruption of the cosmos.

'Arms will be made out of copper;
bread shall be demanded with blood;
one shall laugh with a sick man's laugh;
one shall not weep at death;

[6] Two gods representing the waters of chaos.

one shall not spend the night fasting for death,
a man's heart concerned with himself alone.
One shall not make mourning today, the heart turning from it
   entirely.
A man shall sit, turning his back
while someone is killing another.
I shall show you a son as a foe,
a brother as an enemy,
a man killing his own father.

Every mouth is full of "I want",
all goodness has fled.
The land perishes, though laws are decreed against it,
for destruction is what is done,
and loss is what is found,
and what is done is what should be undone:
a man's goods have been taken from him, and given to the
   outsider.
I shall show you the master in trouble(?)
and the outsider at rest,
one who did nothing helping himself
and one who did in want.
Hating, one will give goods to silence a mouth that speaks,
and a speech is answered with an arm going out with a stick,
and one speaks with slaughter.

Words are like fire to the heart;
what comes from the mouth cannot be endured.
Shrunk is the land, many its controllers.
It falls apart – its taxes are great.
Little is the corn; large is the measure,
and it is measured out with overflowing.
Re withdraws himself from mankind.
Though he shall rise when it is time, it shall not be known when
   midday occurs;
there is no one who can distinguish his shadow, no one's face is
   bright when (he) is glimpsed;
no one's eyes are moist with water.
He is in the sky (but) like the moon;
his accustomed times shall not stray,
(but) his rays on the face are (now) events of the past.

I shall show you the land in a state of suffering,
the weak as the lord of force,
and the one once greeted greeting.
I shall show you the lowermost uppermost,
one who did service now one who turns about a generation.

One shall live in the necropolis.
The wretched will make wealth;
the great will pay respect to exist.
It is the poor who will eat bread,
while servants are exalted.
The Heliopolitan nome will not exist for the land –
the birthplace of every god.'

3 An exile's longing for the State: from the 'Tale of Sinuhe'

The 'Tale of Sinuhe' is one of the supreme masterpieces of Egyptian literature. Five manuscripts are known from the Middle Kingdom, and numerous ostraca from the school at Deir el-Medineh show that it enjoyed the status of a 'classic' in the New Kingdom. The most complete manuscript dates to the period around Amenemhat III, and was part of a literary library placed in the 12th-Dynasty Theban tomb (the 'Berlin library': see also **14, 50**). The next most complete comes from a 13th-Dynasty tomb on the west bank at Thebes, where it was found in a chest with twenty-two other papyri, now known as the 'Ramesseum Papyri', which included magical and medical texts (**14, 18, 30, 45**); these, with the magical equipment also discovered there, suggest that the owner was a lector priest.

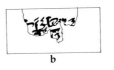

b

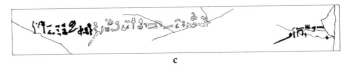

c

a

Lines from the 'Tale of Sinuhe'. The three copies show the changing styles of hieratic: (a) is the manuscript from the mid-12th Dynasty 'Berlin library'; (b) is the fragmentary copy from the 'Ramesseum' archive, 13th Dynasty; (c) is the Ramessid copy with rubrics on the massive ostracon (32 × 89 cm), now in the Ashmolean Museum, Oxford. All came from Thebes. (Not to scale.)

The tale, spanning the reigns of Amenemhat I and Senwosret I, is the fictional autobiography of a courtier who flees Egypt in panic at the death of the old king (see **9**) and who eventually returns to be buried in honour beside Senwosret. A major theme is the contrast between the ideal order of Egyptian life and the unstructured existence of the Palestinian tribesmen. In these dramatic verses, which are from the turning-point of the tale, Sinuhe rejoices at the success he has achieved in exile, but his lyrical exultation breaks down into an urgent prayer as he realises the futility of this. Life is meaningful and enduring only within the State, whose values are here represented by the king and Egyptian ritual.

'For god has acted to be gracious to one with whom he was
    angry,

whom he led astray to another country.
Today, he is satisfied.
A fugitive flees his surroundings,
while my report is in the Residence.
A laggard lags for hunger,
while I give bread to my neighbour.
A man abandons his land for nakedness,
while I have bright, white linen.
A man runs off for lack of someone to send,
while I have many serfs.
Goodly is my house, spacious my dwelling place,
and memory of me is in the palace.
Yet, whatever god ordained this exile – be gracious,
and bring me home!
Surely you will let me see the place where my heart still stays!
What matters more than my being buried
in a land where I was born?
This is my cry for help, that the good event befall,
that god give me grace!
May he act so, to make well the end of one whom he afflicted,
his heart sore for one whom he drove away
to live in a foreign country.
Today, is he gracious, that he shall hear the prayer of one far
off,
who would turn back from where he has roamed the earth,
back to the place from which he was carried off?

May the king of Egypt be gracious to me,
that I may live on his grace.
May I greet the Mistress of the Land who is in his palace,
and hear the behests of her children. Then may my limbs grow
young again,
for old age has descended;
weakness has overtaken me,
my eyes are heavy and my arms faint;
my legs fail to follow, my heart weary:
I am near to death!
May they conduct me to the Cities of Eternity,[1]
may I follow the Lady to the Limit,
Then may she tell me that all is well with her children;
may she traverse eternity over me!'

---

[1] The necropolis.

The king

The role of the king was central to Egyptian culture (see p.28). He was its definition, and its history was his actions. His absolute political authority mirrored the uniqueness of the creator god's governance, and his function partook of the divine: thus he was the god's 'son', 'heir', 'image', even a 'god' himself. As such, he was the sole intermediary between the world of the divine and of men (**4**). In monumental texts describing historical events he alone was the initiator of action (**5**), which was always in accordance with the divine will and always a manifestation of the eternal design. In political terms he was the defender of the State, an omnipotent warrior against enemies (**6**), the maintainer of social order and the protector of the poor (**7**).

History was ideally a direct, uniform sequence of such perfect figures extending from the time of the creator to the present (**8**), but reality is never thus, and the 12th Dynasty followed a particularly extensive time of conflict. This dichotomy between the ideal and actual was explored in literary texts which examined both the divine and the fallible aspects of a single king, and from these it is clear that kings were not considered to be above ethical judgement, but were subject to the same universal laws of retribution and reciprocity as the rest of mankind (**9, 10**). The humanity of the king found expression particularly in tales; the final text (**11**) presents a king who is a man capable of behaving scandalously.

4 The king and his cosmic role: 'The King as Sun-priest'

One of the 18th-Dynasty rooms in the temple at Luxor contains a cryptically arranged version of a text which is found in other temples and tombs of the New Kingdom and Late Period, having been adopted by private individuals for funerary use. In its original form it is an unusually descriptive text about the king worshipping the rising sun, which at Luxor forms an extended caption on a scene of King Amenhotep III before the solar bark. The language and orthography suggest a composition date before the end of the Middle Kingdom, although these features may be later archaisms.

The first section comprises two stanzas which concern the sunrise, and the second presents the king as the possessor of arcane and mystical knowledge. The resonant lines of the third form an unusually explicit analysis of the king's rule in relation to the gods, men and the dead, acting out Re's creation of Truth on earth. His role of intermediary is thematically linked to the context of the whole, for sunrise is a transition from the world of the divine to the 'land of the living'. The expression of the communion of the two worlds reaches a climax at the conclusion, when the king is likened to the god he is worshipping.

King N
praises Re at dawn,
at his coming forth, as he opens up his primordial egg
and climbs to heaven as Khepri:[1]

He enters at the mouth;
he comes forth from the thighs[2]
at his manifestations of the east of heaven,
as his father Osiris raises him,
as the arms of Heh and Hehet receive him,[3]
as he comes to rest in the Morning bark.

King N knows
this secret speech which the eastern Souls[4] say,
as they sing acclamations to Re
as he rises and appears in the horizon;
the bolts open for him
in the portals of the eastern horizon,
so that he shall sail on the ways of the sky.
He knows their secret images, their forms,
their towns which are in God's land.
He knows the place where they stand
at Re's setting forth.
He knows that speech
which the crews say when they drag the bark of the Horizon
    Dweller.
He knows the manifestations of Re
and his forms which are in the flood.
He knows this secret portal, through which the great god
    comes forth.
He knows he who is in the Morning Bark,
the great leader in the Evening bark.
He knows your fields in the horizon,
your courses which are in heaven.

Re has placed King N
in the land of the living
for eternity and all time;
for judging men, for making the gods content,
for creating Truth, for destroying evil.

---

[1] The first of several metaphors for the sun's daily progress: a scarab hatching from a ball of dung.

[2] The sky is a goddess who swallows the sun at night and gives birth at dawn.

[3] The sun is lifted from the realm of Osiris, and then into the sky by its supporters, the god and goddess of space.

[4] Mythical beings, who were portrayed as apes chattering at dawn.

He gives offerings to the gods,
and invocation offerings to the blessed spirits.
The name of king N is
in heaven like Re.
He lives in joy,
like Re Harakhti,
at seeing whom the patricians rejoice,
for whom the folk make jubilations,
in his form of Youth.

The coming forth of Re as Khepri.[5]

5 A royal act: the building inscription of Senwosret I

From the New Kingdom, there are several texts from stelae and temple walls which were copied on to papyri and writing boards, and circulated beyond their original monumental context. A leather roll of the 18th Dynasty (30 x 46 cm) preserves this text on two pages, with the addition of (sometimes carelessly placed) verse points; the original was almost certainly carved on a stela (or wall) in the temple at Heliopolis. Few such royal texts are attested from the Middle Kingdom, due at least in part to the later rebuilding of the sites.

The description of the ritual foundation of a monument at Heliopolis is an example of the so-called *Königsnovellen* which described various kinds of royal activity; the act is usually a single great deed, and its presentation is structured by a dialogue between the king and the courtiers, including a self-eulogy and eulogy. Here it accommodates explicit mention of the king's acting through a deputy (a practical necessity), although its main concern is to present the king as the agent of the divine, acting 'for eternity'. The genre can be related to literary narratives about kings, in which a council scene is a well-attested motif, and it displays considerable variety in the New Kingdom.

The actual temple site is not well preserved, but features an obelisk erected by Senwosret I; this was probably part of these works:

Year 3, month 3 of Akhet, day 8,
under the Person of the Dual King: Kheperkare,
Son of Re: Senwosret {true of voice},
may he live for all time and eternity.

The king appeared in the double-crown;
an enthronement occurred in the Hall, and a consultation with
    his followers,
the Friends of the Palace l.p.h.,
and the officials of the private chambers.
Commands at their hearing,
a consultation for their instruction:
'Look, my Person is planning works,
being mindful of a deed of excellence;
for the future I shall make a monument.

The red granite obelisk of Senwosret I at Heliopolis (H. 2,040 cm). The inscription records his titulary and mentions his jubilee.

[5] A concluding caption, rather than part of the text proper.

I shall lay down durable decrees for Harakhti,
as he bore me for doing what should be done for him, for
   creating what he commanded done.
He has set me to be shepherd of this land;
he knew who would gather it together for him.
He has handed to me what he guards, what the eye which is
   with him illumines.
He who does even as he desires,
I have [acquired(?)] what he has ordained to be known.
I am a king by virtue of my being,
a sovereign to whom (the office) is not given;
as a fledgling I conquered;
I lorded in the egg;
I controlled as a youth.
He enriched me, to be the lord of my two shares[1]
as a lad, not yet loosed from swaddling clothes.
He appointed me to be lord of the folk,
created before the sunfolk.
He brought me up to be the one in the palace
as a weanling, not yet out from the thighs.
The land was given to me,
its length and breadth;
I have been nursed as a born conqueror.
The land was given to me; I am its lord.
My power has reached the heights of heaven,
one excellent of aspect through acting for my maker,
one who contents god with what he gave.
I am his son, his protector;
he ordained for me conquest of what he conquered.

I am come as Horus, having come of age,
having established offering loaves for the gods, that I may
   make a work
in the great mansion of (my) father Atum.
He shall enrich himself, even as he has caused me to conquer.
I shall provision his altars upon earth.
I shall build my mansion in his neighbourhood.
My goodness shall be remembered in his house;
the pyramidion(?) is my name;
the lake is my monument.
To do excellence is eternity.
A king who is evoked on account of his achievements cannot
   die;
transience(?) can not know him who plans for himself,
as his name is still pronounced.

---

[1] The shares are the 'two lands'.

The affairs of all time do not perish.
What is is what is made;
it is probing out excellence.
A name is good provision;
it is being vigilant about the affairs of eternity.'

And these Royal Friends said,
making answers to their god:
'Utterance is ⟨in⟩ your mouth, and Perception round you!
O sovereign l.p.h., what occurs is your plan:
the royal appearance as the uniter of the two lands
to st[retch the cord] in your temple.
It is noble to look to tomorrow,
as something excellent for one's lifetime.
The populace cannot profit without you,
as your Person is the eyes of everyone.
Great are you, as you make monuments
in On, the sanctuary of the gods,
before your father, the lord of the Great Mansion,
Atum, the bull of the ennead.
Create your mansion; provide for the offering stone,
that it shall do service for the statue
and be well disposed to your image
for the fullness of all time.'

The king himself said:
'Royal Seal-bearer, Sole Friend,
Overseer of the two Gold-houses and two Silver-houses,
and Master of the Secrets of the Two Crowns,
it is your counsel which causes to be made all the works
which my Person has desired to exist.
You are the master of them,
he who shall do as I wish.
Art and vigilance,
they exist for him who is free of slackness.
All works belong to the instructed.
The maker of excellence is the lord of deeds;
your hour is a time of action.
[It is broa]d according to your manner of decreeing things.
Make the place whose creation is desired!
Decree to the workmen
to work according to what you have ordained!'

Appearance of the king in the Two-plumed Diadem, with all
   the folk around him,
with the lector priest and chief, and the scribe of the divine
   book stretching the cord.

The rope was let loose, the line put on the ground,
and made into this mansion.
And then his Person caused (them) to proceed;
the king turned himself back to face the people,
who were joined together in one place,
(both) Upper and Lower Egypt,
they who are in prosperity upon earth.[2]

6 The presentation of military power: the boundary stela of Senwosret III

This stela dates from the sixteenth year of Senwosret III (1846 BC) and was set up in the shrine of the recently established frontier fortress of Semna, overlooking the Nile at the southern end of the second cataract. The stela is of red granite (150 x 80 cm), with a round top; below a representation of a winged sun disc the text is carved in twenty-one horizontal lines of hieroglyphs. It was discovered in two pieces by Lepsius in 1844, but the upper half was forgotten on the river bank while it was being shipped to Berlin, and lay there for forty years before being rediscovered and reunited with the lower half. A duplicate of the stela was also erected at the fortress of Uronarti.

The text which opens with the formal royal titulary, records Senwosret's eulogy of his own power over the local Nubians; stylistically, epithet is piled upon epithet forming a grandiloquent sequence typical of the genre. In the concluding section he expects his successors to maintain his achievement, and addresses the audience (presumably the commanders of the fortress) to do likewise. In this they are inspired by his 'image', a statue of the king within the shrine, which was probably similar to the example illustrated.

Horus: Divine of Forms;
Two Ladies: Divine of Manifestations;
Dual King: Khakaure given life;
Golden Horus: Being;
Re's Bodily Son, whom he loves,
the Lord of the Two Lands: Senwosret,
given life, stability, power for all time!
Year 16, month 3 of Peret:
his Person's making the southern boundary at Semna.

I have made my boundary, out-southing my forefathers.
I have exceeded what was handed down to me.
I am a king, whose speaking is acting;
what happens by my hand is what my heart plans;
one who is aggressive to capture,
swift to success;
who sleeps not with a matter (still) in his heart;
who takes thought for dependants, and stands by mercy;
who is unmerciful to the enemy that attacks him;
who attacks when attacked,
and is quiet when it is quiet;
who responds to a matter as it happens.

---

[2] The final section alone concerns the actual laying-out and foundation of the monument. The copy proceeds no further, but it is uncertain whether this was the end of the original inscription.

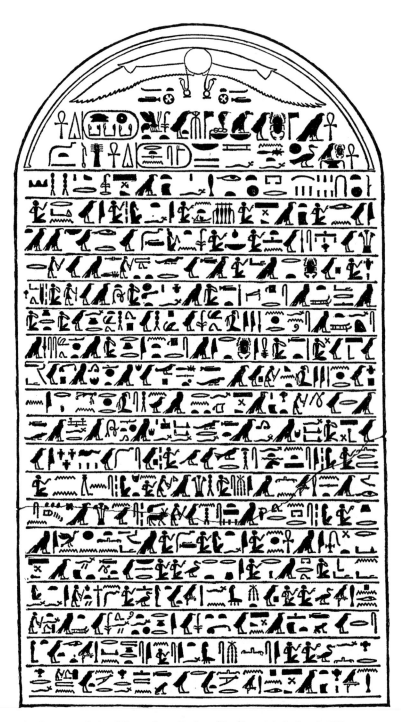

The Semna stela (H. 150 cm; from Budge, *The Egyptian Sudan*, I, 545.

For he who is quiet after attack,
he is making the enemy's heart strong.
Aggression is bravery;
retreat is vile.
He who is driven from his boundary is a true back-turner,
since the Nubian only has to hear to fall at a word:
answering him makes him retreat.
One is aggressive to him and he shows his back;
retreat and he becomes aggressive.
Not people to be respected –
they are wretches, broken-hearted!
My Person has seen it – it is not an untruth;
for I have plundered their women, and carried off their
   underlings,
gone to their wells, driven off their bulls,
torn up their corn, and put fire to it.

A black granite statue of Senwosret III (BM 686; H. 122 cm). This rugged portrait came from Deir el-Bahri, Thebes.

45

As my father lives for me,[1]
I speak true;
here is no boastful phrase
which has come from my mouth.

Now, as for any son of mine who shall make firm this boundary
    my Person made,
he is my son, born of my Person;
the son who vindicates his father is a model,
making firm the boundary of his begetter.
Now as for him who shall neglect it, shall not fight for it –
no son of mine, not born to me!
Now my Person has caused an image of my Person to be made,
upon this boundary which my Person made,
so that you shall be firm for it, so that you shall fight for it.

7 The king as protector: a hymn to Senwosret III

This is the third of a cycle of five hymns to Senwosret III which was found in the pyramid town of el-Lahun (see p.29, **28**) and was probably part of a temple archive there. The hymns were perhaps intended for recitation at a royal visit or, more probably, at a ritual as part of a royal cult in the temple.

The hymn is structured by a refrain which is copied out once, with the rest of the stanzas written as single indented lines. It extols the royal power as a personal force; in it the central authority assumes the role of a local ruler. The metaphors are frequently intimate and domestic, but they also embrace State and cosmic protection, and the last assimilates the royal guardian with the divine.

How great is the lord of his city:
he is unique and millionfold;
a thousand other men are little!

The hymn to Senwosret III, showing the strophic arrangement. The hand is a good example of mid-12th-Dynasty literary hieratic (H. 7 cm; from Möller, *Hier. Lesestücke* I, 5 c).

---

[1] 'As the king lives for me' was the formula used in swearing an oath.

How great is the lord of his city:
lo, he is a dyke,
damming the river, against its flood of waters!

How great is the lord of his city:
lo, he is a chamber,
letting a man sleep till dawn!

How great is the lord of his city:
lo, he is a rampart,
walled with copper of Sinai!

How great is the lord of his city:
lo, he is a refuge,
whose hold does n[ot] slip!

How great is the lord of his city:
lo, he is a shelter,
rescuing the fearful from his enemies!

How great is the lord of his city:
lo, he is an overflowing shade,
cool in summer!

How great is the lord of his city:
lo, he is a warm corner,
dry in the wintertime!

How great is the lord of his city:
lo, he is a mountain,
shutting out the gale at the time of the sky's storm!

How great is the lord of his city:
lo, he is a Sekhmet
against his enemies who have trodden on his boundaries!

8 Kings in history: a king-list

Egyptian historiography is epitomised by the 'king-list' – a catalogue of royal names and reign lengths. An early example of this tradition is this graffito in Wadi Hammamat, carved by people whose titles indicate that they were part of a mining expedition. The incised hieroglyphs are clumsy, often being shaped as if hieratic, and the text, though short, is full of bizarre spellings and orthographies. Although there is no date, and the only dated graffito in that area refers to a King Sobekhotep of the 13th Dynasty, the palaeography is suggestive of some time in the 12th. The contents accord with this, for in the Middle Kingdom the court of the 4th Dynasty attracted much interest and featured in several literary texts. These Memphite goldsmiths commemorated the ancient kings, but betrayed the limitations of their historical knowledge: only the first three were actually successive kings, the last two being princes.

The king-list graffito from the Wadi Hammamat (dimensions unrecorded).

> Dual King,
> given life
> for all time: Khufu; Redjedef; Khafre; Hordjedef{re}(sic);
> Bauefre.
> The goldsmith of Ptah, Nunu; the porter, Hotepiu; the
> goldsmith of Ptah, Khenu;
> the porter of wooden rollers(?) Remeni.

9 The royal burden: the 'Teaching of Amenemhat I'

This teaching was regarded as a classic text during the New Kingdom, when numerous school-copies were made on ostraca (over seventy). Although careful copies on papyri and writing boards provide more consistently valuable evidence for piecing together the text, it remains particularly fragmentary at the end.

The teaching is spoken, Hamlet-like, by the dead Amenemhat I, as his son assumes the throne; a Ramessid eulogy of the scribe Khety (**60b**), however, makes it clear that it actually was composed by him during the reign of Senwosret I. In the context of a dynastic crisis the text must have had some political overtones although its treatment of the two kings is not propagandistic; rather, it is an intensely dramatic monologue, which characterises Amenemhat as both an embittered old man and an ideal ruler, interweaving the universal themes of the divinity and humanity of the king.

After an initial injunction to his son to rule, Amenemhat warns him against treachery and calls on the people to vindicate his memory. He then describes the fatal attack, which caught him in an unguarded moment, alone and vulnerable. In self-justification, the unexpected-ness of the violence is demonstrated by his previous supremacy, manifested in an autobiographical account of the reign, whose calm grand style differs from the tone of the preceding stanzas. This climaxes in the sumptuous mansion which embodies the permanence of his achievements (either his palace or his tomb). A contrasting image of people disputing in the streets outside brings back the actuality of the crisis, and the king's ghost is torn away from his son. As he departs, he enjoins Senwosret to rise to the divinity of the kingship.

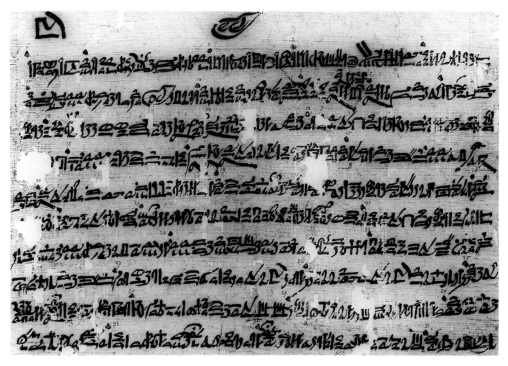

A New Kingdom copy of the opening of the 'Teaching of Amenemhat'. The roll (BM 10182 = Papyrus Sallier 2) contains a collection of Middle Kingdom texts and shows a fine 19th-Dynasty hand (H. 16 cm). Above the top line are added the correct forms of two signs which the scribe had not copied perfectly. According to the colophon the scribe was Inene, and the teacher Qageb, treasury officials of Seti II (1204–1198 BC).

BEGINNING OF THE TEACHING
made by the Person of the Dual King: Sehotepibre;
Son of Re: Amenemhat, true of voice,
when he spoke in a revelation
to his son, the Lord to the Limit.
He said 'Rise as a god!
Listen to what I tell you,
that you may rule the land, and govern the Banks,
increasing the good.

Gather yourself against subjects who do not (really) exist,
whose respect cannot be trusted;
do not approach them when you are alone!
Trust no brother; know no friend!
Make for yourself no intimates – there is no profit in this!

May you sleep, having yourself guarded your heart,

for there will be no serfs for a man
on the day of pain.
I gave to the poor, raised the orphan,
and caused him who had not to end up like him who had.

It was one who ate my provisions that made insurrection;
one to whom I had given my arms was creating plots with
    them;
one clad in my linen was looking at me as if needy;
one anointed with my myrrh was passing water.[1]

O my living images, my partners among men,
make for me mourning, such as has not been heard!
An abundance of fighting, such as has not been seen!
When one fights in the arena, forgetful of the past,
there is no profit in the goodness of him who ignores what he
    should know.[2]

It was after supper, when night had fallen,
and I had spent an hour of happiness.
I was asleep upon my bed, having become weary,
and my heart had begun to follow sleep.
When weapons of my counsel were wielded,
I had become like a snake of the necropolis.

As I came to, I awoke to fighting,
and I found that it was an attack of the bodyguard.
If quickly I had taken weapons in my hand,
I would have made the buggers retreat with a charge.
But there is none mighty in the night,
none who can fight alone;
no success will come without a helper.

Look, my injury happened while I was without you,
when the entourage had not yet heard that I would hand over
    to you,
when I had not yet sat with you, that I might make counsels for
    you;
for I did not plan it, I did not foresee it,
and my heart had not taken thought of the negligence of
    servants.

Had any woman previously raised troops?
Is tumult raised in the Residence?

---

[1] A gesture of disrespect or an idiom for making complaints?

[2] i.e., no good will result from even well-intentioned actions made in ignorance of the truth.

Is water which destroys the earth let forth?
Are commoners deceived by what they have done?[3]
Evil had not come around me, since my birth;
the like of my deed as a valiant hero had not occurred.

I went to Elephantine,
and I travelled to the Delta;
I stood on the limits of the land, having seen its midst.
The limits of strength I reached,
with my strong arm, and my forms.

I was a maker of corn, beloved of Nepri.
On every plain the Inundation paid respect to me.
No one hungered in my years; no one thirsted then.
Men relaxed through what I had done, and told of me.
All that I decreed was as it should be.

I subjugated the lions; I captured crocodiles.
I subdued the Nubians; I captured Medjai;
I made the Asiatics do the dog-walk.[4]

I made for myself a mansion decorated with electrum,
and its portals were of lapis-luzuli,
with walls of silver,
a floor of sycamore,
doors of copper,
bolts of bronze,
made for all time,
prepared for eternity.
I know, for I was the lord thereof, to the limit!

Yet, the offspring of many are in the street,
the wise saying "yes",
the fool "no",
for he knows not himself, he who lacks your sight.
O Senwosret, my son!
My feet are departing, even as my very heart draws near,
and my eyes are looking for you –
the offspring of a joyous hour,
beside the sunfolk, who were praising you!

---

[3] The rhetorical questions imply that the attack, which probably originated in the harem, could not have
been foreseen. The sense of the last is perhaps: how could I have expected such deceptive treachery,
which is not practised even on commoners, let alone on a king?

[4] i.e., crawl submissively.

Look, I have made the beginning, that I might tie up the end for
  you.
It is I who has brought to land for you what was in my heart:
my likeness, wearing the White Crown, divine progeny!
This is as it should be, as I decreed for you.
In the bark of Re I have descended;[5]
arise to the kingship created aforetime,
it being what I made, in the midst of (all) this![6]
Set up monuments, endow your funerary buildings!
May you fight for the wisdom the heart knows,
for you want it beside your Person!'

IT IS COME, WELL AND IN PEACE[7]

10 The fallibility of the king: from the 'Teaching for Merikare'

The name of the teacher of King Merikare is not fully preserved in any of the three 18th-Dynasty manuscripts, the principal of which is Papyrus Lenigrad 1116a, but he may well have been King Khety Nebkaure. The date of this teaching is unclear (perhaps the 11th or early 12th Dynasty); it is set vividly in the troubled Heracleopolitan period, which forms the background for a bleak discourse on the duties of kingship, and also on the workings of retribution.

In these stanzas from the conclusion, King Khety presents the solitary uniqueness of the ruler, and mentions the desecration of the necropolis at Abydos which occurred during his conflicts with the emerging 11th Dynasty. For this there was retribution – perhaps fatal, as he seems to speak from the grave – but he sees that this misfortune can be a sign that god, although invisible and transcendent, still tends the world. The passage ends with a eulogistic affirmation of divine care for mankind, which is manifested throughout creation, even in its suffering. Even the creator's partial destruction of mankind sprang from a paternal concern (see p.31). Similarly, the king, although flawed, is shown still to be an embodiment, albeit incomplete, of the supreme Good Shepherd. The concept of knowledge in particular is used to articulate this theme: the king should be a sage, but was only partially aware of events, while the aloof god is omniscient.

'The ‹Lord› of the Two Banks is a sage;
the King, lord of courtiers, cannot be foolish.
At his coming forth from the womb he was wise,
and god has distinguished him before a million (other) men.

Kingship is a goodly office;
it has no son, it has no brother, who could make your
  monument endure:
it is the individual man who restores another.

[5] The dead king has entered the world of the gods.

[6] i.e., even in the midst of such troubles.

[7] The New Kingdom version of the colophon found in literary manuscripts. The original would have read:

  IT IS COME FROM BEGINNING TO END,
  AS FOUND IN WRITING.

A man shall act for his predecessor
for the sake of what he did being restored by another
    succeeding him.
Look, a vile deed happened in my time:
The nome of Thinis was destroyed.
Not as my action it happened,
and I knew of it (only) after it was done.
See my fault, beyond what I did.
Now, destruction is vile.
There is no good for a man in refurbishing what he has
    destroyed,
in restoring what he has defaced – beware of it![1]
With its like is a blow repaid:
all that is done is bound together.

Generation passes generation of men,
and god, who knows the character (of men), has hidden
    himself.
Yet there can be no opposing the Lord of the Hand:
he is one who attacks what eyes can see.
Respect shall be shown to god on his path,
made of jewels, fashioned of copper,
like a flood repaid with a flood:
no river lets itself be concealed,
but is the opener of the course in which it hid itself.[2]
Even thus, the soul goes back to the place it knows;
it cannot stray from the paths of yesterday.
Make worthy your mansion of the west,
establish your place of the necropolis,
with righteousness, with doing Truth, on which their[3] hearts
    rely.
The character of the right-hearted shall be accepted
against the ox of the evil-doer.
Act for god, and just so shall he act for you,
– with offerings for a flourishing altar, and carvings.
This a guidance for your name;
god is aware of who acts for him.

Tended is mankind, the cattle of god.
For their sakes he made heaven and earth,
and drove off the Rapacity of the waters.
So that their nostrils should breathe he made the winds.

[1] i.e., beware of thinking that the consequences of a crime can be avoided.

[2] The ways of god are as irresistible as a flood.

[3] i.e., the gods' hearts.

They are images of him, come forth from his flesh.
For their sakes he rises in heaven.
So that they should eat he made
plants and flocks, fowl and fish.
He has slaughtered his enemies; he has destroyed his children,
for their thinking of making rebellion.

For their sake he shines.
To see them he sails.
He has set up for himself a shrine around them.
They weep and he is listening.
He has made for them rulers from birth,
commanders to raise
in the back of the weak.[4]
He has made for them magic, as a weapon
to oppose the blow of events,
watching over them, night and day.
He has slaughtered the disaffected amongst them,
like a man smiting his son for his brother.
God knows every name.'

11 The king in folklore: the 'Tale of King Neferkare and General Sasenet'

The tale is known from three very fragmentary manuscripts, spanning a period of some 650 years: a writing board from the late 18th Dynasty, a Theban papyrus from the 25th Dynasty, and a 20th-Dynasty ostracon from the village of Deir el-Medineh. Clearly, the popularity of the tale was extensive. Internal details, together with linguistic features in these late copies, suggest that the original may have been composed at the end of the Middle Kingdom. In style it is similar to the well-known 'Tales from the Court of King Khufu' in Papyrus Westcar, which dates to the Second Intermediate Period, and both compositions exemplify an apparently more 'popular' form of literature than most Middle Kingdom narratives. Like Papyrus Westcar and **8**, this tale reflects the period's interest in Old Kingdom royalty.

As with so many Egyptian sources, these copies are insufficient for a full reconstruction of the original. In the opening fragment the scene is set in the reign of a king Neferkare, perhaps Pepy II (2246–2152 BC). Iti the patrician was perhaps described as helping, or at least knowing of, the king's desire for his general. In the second fragment a man from Memphis, the capital of the Old Kingdom, seems to be trying to denounce the general (and presumably the king) before various members of the court, who ignore him. Whenever he tries, his petition is cunningly drowned by court musicians. In fragment 3 a man of rank called Tjeti appears; he has probably been informed of the affair by the pleader in the intervening lost section. He follows the king on one of his amorous visits, and confirms the report of the affair; he is the first recorded amateur detective. The ending is difficult to imagine. The king's behaviour is not presented favourably, and other sources show that homosexuality was viewed as an aberration from the ideal standard of family life, similar to adultery. The tale may well have ended with the king abandoning his affair and being forced into more decorous behaviour.

---

[4] i.e., to force them to be strong?

(Fragment 1)
It happened that the Person of the Dual King: Neferkare;
Son of Re: [Pepy], true of voice,
was beneficent king in this entire land.
Now, the Patrician and [Count, the ...] of his Person,
the [....] called Iti
[..... knew of (?)] the love [of the king]
[for] General Sasenet,
in whose [entire house] there was no wife.
General Sasenet went out,
to take a walk for pleasure
[.......................]
[............ King] Teti,[1] {as} true of voice [.......]

(Fragment 2)
[......] General Sasenet.
And he discussed [...... the love(?) of]
[the Person of the Dual King:] Neferkare.
General Sasenet went out
[............. with(?)]
the Great [...] of the King, the Overseer of [...]
the High Steward, the Overseer of the Chamber,
the [....], the [......],
the Royal Scribe, the Journeyman of the Scribe of Royal
     Documents,
the Overseer of Fields, the [...], the [....],
the courtiers of the Residence
and the council of Memphis,
without [listening to the Pleader of Memphis].
Now, the Pleader of Memphis,
arrived at the [...],
but he was [prevented(?)] by the singers' songs, the musicians'
     music,
the acclaimers' acclamations and the whistlers' whistling,
until the Pleader of Memphis went out [from there];
(then) they stopped, [having not listened to him].
If the Pleader of Memphis came
to speak before the Overseer of the Court,
he made the singers sing, the musicians make music,
the acclaimers acclaim, and the whistlers whistle,
until the Pleader of Memphis left without them hearing;
(then) they stopped booing him.
The Pleader of Memphis left,

---

[1] The most probable restoration is that Sasenet is described as walking past a funerary monument or estate of the earlier King Teti (2323–2291 BC) in the region of Memphis.

weeping very greatly;
his hair was [torn out],
[................]

(Fragment 3)
[................]
[Hent's son Tjeti .....]
[................].
Then he noticed the Person of the Dual King: Neferkare
going out at night,
all alone, with nobody with him.
Then he removed himself from him, without letting him see.
Hent's son Tjeti stood,
thinking: 'So this is it!
What was said is true –
he goes out at night.'
Hent's son Tjeti went,
just behind this god –
without letting his heart misgive him – to see all that he did.
He (Neferkare) arrived
at the house of General Sasenet.
Then he threw a brick, and kicked (the wall),
so that a [ladder(?)] was let down for him.
Then he ascended,
while Hent's son Tjeti
waited until his Person returned.
Now after his Person had done what he desired with him,[2]
he returned to his palace, and Tjeti went behind him.
When his Person returned to the palace l.p.h.,
Tjeti went (back) to his house.
Now, his Person went to the house
of General Sasenet
when four hours had passed of the night,
he had spent another four hours in the house
of General Sasenet,
and he entered the palace
when there were four hours to dawn.
And Hent's son Tjeti went
[following] him each night – without his heart misgiving him;
and (each time,) after his Person entered [the palace]
[Tjeti went (back) to his house ......]

---

[2] i.e., made love to Sasenet.

The physiognomy of an age: the quartzite statue of the 12th-Dynasty official Ankhrenu (BM 1785; H. of head 12 cm).

The life of the land

This section is divided into two parts. The first contains images and descriptions of society (**12–25**) which are self-conscious and to varying degrees idealised. The second comprises actual documents (**26–40**) which provide evidence for the practical workings of society.

Below the king there was the administrative elite, and below them the vast majority of the population. Society was split very unequally, and ninety-nine per cent of the populace is witnessed only in archaeological evidence. A sense of individualism was not prominent, and persons were defined primarily by their social role: in representations this can be seen in the importance of indicators of rank (such as costume) at the expense of 'portraiture', and in texts in the prominence of administrative titles and filiation ('X's son Y'). The family was the basic social unit, rather than a man as an individual; the family was patriarchal and the role of women in society was limited.

Writing inevitably presented society in terms of the elite's activities (**12**), although the responsibility of rank towards the poor was implicit in its social role. Personal virtue was expressed both as finding favour with superiors and looking after inferiors: virtue was knowing how to conform to the standard (**13**). An abuse of power is described in **14**, where an official is accused of wilfully failing to 'do Truth', and perfect behaviour was judged by an absolute standard, not just by conformity to customary behaviour. A union of general social and absolute values is seen in the description of perfect conduct in **15**, which is significantly set in a remote golden age, when ideal and actual were one. The text makes no distinction between private, domestic matters (such as adultery) and public affairs (such as official conduct in court).

The attitude of the elite to the rest of the people was diverse: the responsibilities of high rank and dependency on labourers are forcefully stated in **16**, while **17** shows the scorn of the bureaucracy for the lowly workers. The latter text presents a vivid picture of everyday life, but one dominated by a scribal mentality. The listing of other trades reveals a pattern of thought which runs through the recording of knowledge: the use of word-sequences to structure life into order. The chaos of the tradesmen's lives is arranged into a sequence of scenes which is contrasted with the order of the scribes' profession, just as the knowledge which sets scribes apart is presented in codified form, in encyclopaedic lists of words for elements of the universe, of medical prescriptions and of mathematical problems (**18-20**). This much-desired order is also found in the idealised representations of life on tomb walls, which were composed with a strict awareness of hierarchy, centred around the large figure of the tomb owner (cf. **12** and **21**). There the people were shown paying homage to the official, even as the official did to the king and he to the gods. Lowly activities were shown in a sanitised form – the complaints of the workers are, unrealistically, about not being able to work enough. The harshness of their lives was not allowed to disturb the harmony, and although these are the most widely known images of society, texts such as **16–17** show that the elite's perception of society was more complex. Harmonious and decorous images alone were appropriate for the tombs which have provided most of our evidence. In practice the administrative work, which was eulogised by its officials as embodying utopian longings for an ideal order, may have been resented: one literary text supplies a rare example of an official yearning to escape to a life of perpetual pastoral simplicity (**25**). Although this is not envisaged as an actual possibility, it is a revealing fantasy.

Actual documents give the impression of an intensely ordered State, with records being kept of all administrative activities and expenditures. A comparable image is found in settlement plans of the period, which are highly regimented. The social order which allowed the poor to be protected from oppression also included enforced labour for the 'Office of Labour', one of the administration's main departments (**26, 33**), along with the treasury and the military. The vizier, as the king's agent, held control over the local governments. His involvement included individual appeals (**26**) and the records of a dockyard (**27**), indicating both the level of centralised control from the capital and also the small size of the elite. The State could be run through personal communication. The temple records from el-Lahun (**28**) have a similarly regimented aspect, including all expenditure in the daybooks. Indications of less-than-smooth running are preserved in complaints and letters, and in one a scribe expresses his anger against his superior (**29d**). This is a rare example of anti-social feeling in the surviving record which exalts obedience and conformity.

A similar control was exercised on the limits of the State, with restrictions on travel and trade at the borders. Foreign policy was concerned with resistance to outside threats (as in **6**), but was also aggressive, as in the military campaigns against Nubia in particular (**31**). These raids were apparently not inspired by economic reasons alone, but by a desire to 'extend the borders', to maintain actively the integrity of the State. The same concern is manifest in the pursuit of fugitives from labour duty, who were hunted at least as far as the oases (**33**; see also **39c**).

The remaining documents of this section illustrate life on a more domestic level. The most remarkable of these are the letters of Heqanakht (**34**). The primacy of sons in his family is clear, as is the extended nature of the family group; a more nuclear family was probably restricted to the high elite, where a son could afford to establish an independent household (see **15**, maxim 21). The letters are dominated by practical concerns, such as property. Personal relationships are more often expressed in letters to the dead, which are concerned with re-establishing the relationships taken for granted amongst the living (**55–7**). Heqanakht's attitude to women echoes that advised by literary texts, where they were portrayed as dutiful domestics or sources of trouble (e.g., **15**, maxims 18 and 21). The letters that survive tended to be required by exceptional circumstances, and so most of their references to relationships are to quarrels and upsets which threaten the running of a family. The same is true of wills and legal records, as there was probably little need to record a transfer officially if there was no chance of a disruption or complication in the succession (**36–7**). Similar circumstances probably produced a record of the size of a soldier's family from el-Lahun, which throws valuable light on the composition of a family (**38**). Glimpses of unexceptional and unidealised domestic life are very rare. Household animals were represented in the tombs, and these can provide a sense of intimacy with ancient everyday life; a list of some dogs' names is included here (**39**).

The final text (**40**) is the monument to a family retainer, which contains a rare and intense expression of affection.

12 The ideal life of society: from the 'Lament of Ipuur'

The 'Lament of Ipuur' is preserved in a fragmentary 19th-Dynasty papyrus (L. 370 cm), apparently from Saqqara. It is a copy, with verse points, of a composition whose date has aroused much controversy; the text may have been edited in the course of transmission. However, its style suggests that it belongs to the late Middle Kingdom, perhaps to the early 13th Dynasty.

The sage Ipuur describes the land as engulfed by chaos (cf. **2**) to a figure of supreme authority, either the creator god or his representative. In the lost sections the 'Lord to the Limit' apparently answered the sage's admonition that evil and suffering had been allowed to triumph (this reply may have resembled the creator's declaration in **1**, and the justification of authority in **10**). Amid the ornate descriptions of disorder are two sections which evoke the happy times that are lost; one is translated here (for the other see **43**):

'Yet it is good, when boats sail south [.........],
[.............],
[without any thieves] robbing them.

Yet it is good, when [.............],
[.............].

Yet it is good, when the net is drawn in,
and birds are tied up [....].

Yet it is good, when [.....]
[......] dignities(?) for them,
and the roads are passable.

Yet it is good, when mens' hands build pyramids,
when pools are dug and plantations are made
with trees for the gods.

Yet it is good, when men are drunk,
when they drink *Miit* and their hearts are happy.

Yet it is good, when shouting is in mouths,
and the magnates of estates stand
watching the shouting from their houses(?),
clad in a linen cloak,
purified in front, (well-)established within(?).

Yet it is good, when beds are made ready,
with the headrests of officials safely set up;
when the need of every man is filled
with a blanket in the shade,
when a door is shut for him who slept in a bush.

Yet it is good, when fine linen is spread out
on New Year's Day, [....] on the bank,
and fine linen is spread out
and linen cloaks are on the ground.
[................]'

13 The ideal life of an individual: the stela of Intef

This stela (66 x 37 cm) is one of three which Intef, a chamberlain of Senwosret I, erected in his fine cenotaph at Abydos (for this phenomenon see **53**). In the upper register Intef is represented making a gesture of greeting, presumably to the sanctuary of Abydos; this illustrates a consecration text, in which he praises the holy land of the necropolis. The rest of the stela is divided into sections each containing a stanza of his self-eulogising autobiography, and each beginning with the words 'I was'. This is a formulaic catalogue of ideal virtue rather than an individual account of an actual life, and its image of a civil servant is representative of the period, although the stylistic symmetry is an extreme example of the genre.

Kissing the earth to the Foremost of the Westerners,
seeing the beauty of Wepwawet, by the Chamberlain Intef;
he says: 'Now, as for this chapel I have made
in the desert of Abydos –
O this land of shelter,
the walls which the Lord to the Limit ordained,
a place excellent since the time of Osiris,
which Horus founded for his forefathers,
which the stars in heaven serve,
the mistress of the sunfolk,
to whom the great ones in Busiris come,
the equal to On in blessedness, with which the Lord to the
    Limit is content –
an invocation offering for the blessed one,
the Chamberlain Intef, begotten of Senet!

Above A limestone statue of Intef from his cenotaph at Abydos (BM 461; H. 64 cm). His corpulence is not naturalistic portraiture but indicative of prosperity.

Left The stela of Intef (66 × 37 cm).

I was silent with the wrathful,
one who mingled with the ignorant, for the sake of quelling
   aggression.

I was cool, free from haste,
knowing the outcome, one who foresaw what would come.

I was a speaker in occasions of wrath,
who knew the phrases about which there is anger.

I was lenient, hearing my name,
towards one who told me the state of his heart.

I was collected, kind, merciful,
who quietened the weeper with a kind word.

I was one generous to his dependant,
who did what was excellent for his equal.

I was one exact in the house of his lord,
who knew flattery when spoken.

I was generous, open-handed,
a lord of provisions, free from neglect.

I was a friend to the little,
sweet of charm to the have-not.

I was the carer of the hungry who was without goods,
open-handed to the poor.

I was wise for him who was not,
one who taught a man what was excellent for him.

I was an exact one of the king's house,
who knew what was said in every office.

I was one who harkened, hearing Truth,
who passed over matters of no concern.

I was one sweet to the house of his lord,
remembered for his successful deeds.

I was good within the offices,
patient and free from piggishness.

I was good, not short-tempered,
not one who seizes a man for a remark.

I was righteous, the likeness of a balance,
truly exact like Thoth.

I was firm-footed, excellent of counsel,
one faithful to his benefactor.

I was wise, one who taught himself wisdom,
who took counsel so as to be asked for counsel.

I was one who spoke in the office of Truth,
cleverly spoken in occasions of anxiety.'

14 Relative and absolute justice in society: from the 'Tale of the Eloquent Peasant'

This petition comes from the 'Tale of the Eloquent Peasant', which is preserved in the same two libraries as the 'Tale of Sinuhe' (3), and which is, like it, one of the Middle Kingdom's masterpieces. It was probably written in the middle of the 12th Dynasty, but is set in an earlier troubled time, that of the 10th Dynasty. In it a peasant is robbed by a gentleman, and appeals to the king's High Steward to intervene. He is, however, so eloquent that the High Steward pretends indifference to keep him talking, as he expounds the nature of real and apparent justice. After nine petitions the High Steward finally reveals his attention and restores the peasant's goods. Through the paradoxical plot the text questions social justice and presents this as an analogue to the problem of divine justice.

In this, the eighth petition, the High Steward is denounced for his failure to perform the duty of an official: embodying the eternal ideal of Truth in society. The petition opens with an attack on the High Steward's greed and wealth, and continues in the second stanza with his abuse of authority, by which, however, the peasant is not intimidated. The central stanza forcefully accuses him of being little more than a thief, as he has misused the privileges bestowed on him. The remainder states the case more abstractly, urging him to abide by absolute Truth – which is the only true good – without compromising the ideal. After a couplet describing Truth's impartiality, the peasant attacks his complete indifference to this inspired reformulation of the creator god's ideal. A final quatrain eulogising Truth's immutability closes the petition.

> And this peasant came to appeal to him (the High Steward) an
>   eighth time,
> saying: 'High Steward, my lord!
> One falls for greed far.
> the selfish one is free from success;
> his success belongs to failure.
> You are selfish – it is not for you;
> you steal – it is no good for you,
> you who should have made a man attend to his good deed
>   truly!
> For it is the case that your portion is in your house, and your
>   belly full,
> while the corn measure brims over and overflows,
> so that its excess perishes on the ground.
>
> Seizer of the robbed, taker!
> The officials who were appointed
> to outlaw evil,
> they are (now) a shelter for the predator,
> those officials who were appointed
> to outlaw falsehood.
> (But) your fearfulness does not make me appeal to you; you do
>   not perceive my heart.
> The silent man[1] who turns back to complain to you –
> he does not fear him whom he supplicates,

---

[1] The 'silent' is a common expression for the 'virtuous'.

though no brother of his is summoned against you from the
   street (to support him).

Your plots are in the country,
your wealth in the estate,
your provisions in the storehouse!
Officials are giving to you,
and you are still taking. So are you a robber?
When people are ushered in before you,
and troops are with you, for the division of plots!

Do Truth for the lord of Truth,
the truth of whose Truth is!
O reed, roll, palette of Thoth,[2]
may you avoid doing evil! The goodness of the good man is
   alone good beyond him.
Yet Truth itself is for eternity.
To the necropolis in its doer's hand it descends;
he is entombed, earth joined with him.
But his name is not effaced on earth;
he is remembered for goodness.
It is the standard of god's word.

If it is scales, it tilts not;
if a balance, it is not partial.

Look, I will come, or another will come,
so you shall make accusation;[3] but do not respond
as the accuser of the silent, nor attack one who cannot!
You do not pity, nor suffer, nor (yet) destroy!
You do not repay me for this perfect speech,
coming forth from the mouth of Re himself.
So speak Truth! Do Truth!

For it is mighty, great, enduring;
its revelation shall be found good: it shall conduct to
   blessedness.
There cannot be excess for the standard.
A vile deed cannot reach port, nor the cargo-bearer landfall!'

15 The life of a perfect official: from the 'Teaching of the Vizier Ptahhotep'

The 'Teaching of Ptahhotep' is preserved in two Middle Kingdom manuscripts (Papyrus British Museum 10371/10435 from the mid-12th Dynasty and Papyrus Prisse from the late

---

[2] Writing is used as a metaphor for the high steward's duty of embodying Truth.

[3] i.e., of the gentleman who robbed me.

12th Dynasty), as well as in New Kingdom copies on ostraca and papyri. Although the protagonist is supposedly a vizier under King Isesi of the 5th Dynasty (2388–2356 BC), the text was probably composed early in the Middle Kingdom.

The teaching comprises thirty-seven maxims of varying lengths, with a narrative prologue and a reflective epilogue. The sage's instructions appear deceptively practical, concerning specific problems of conduct and decorum, but these are formulated to exemplify abstract ideals of perfect living and Truth. In the golden past of the setting even 'the eating of bread is according to the counsel of god', and worldly success is the inevitable result of virtue. The 'perfect speech' at which the teaching aims is not a careerist's rhetoric but 'spoken perfection'; that is, Truth embodied in speech. The selection of maxims translated here displays the interwoven texture of pragmatic advice (such as maxim 17) and universal pronouncements (maxim 5), which embraces all spheres of life.

BEGINNING OF THE PHRASES OF PERFECT SPEECH
SPOKEN BY the Patrician and Count,
the eldest King's Bodily Son,
the Lord Vizier Ptahhotep,
in teaching the ignorant to be wise,
to be the standard of perfect speech,
excellent to him who shall listen,
baneful to him who will transgress it.
And he said before his son:

(Maxim 1)
'Be not proud for being wise.
Consult with the ignorant as with the wise.

A model of servants at a millstone and baking bread in moulds; from a Middle Kingdom tomb (BM 45197; L. 42 cm).

The limits of art have not been attained;
there is no artist (fully) equipped with his excellence.
Perfect speech is concealed, more than emerald;
(yet) it is found with the maids at millstones.

(Maxim 5)
If you are a leader,
ordaining the affairs of the multitude,
seek out for yourself every good deed,
so that your affairs shall be faultless.
Great is Truth, enduring is ‹its› effectiveness,
it has not been disturbed since the time of Osiris.
He who transgresses the laws is punished
– it is a transgression (even) in the view of the selfish.
It is baseness which seizes a lifetime of wealth,
but wrong has not yet ever brought its deed to land.[1]
A man says, "I myself will snare,"
but he cannot say, "I will snare because of my occupation."
When the end comes, Truth endures.
Let no man say, "It is my family property."[2]

(Maxim 11)
Follow your heart[3] as long as you live.
Do not do more than is required.
Do not waste the time of following the heart:
it is an abomination to the spirit to destroy it.
Do not reject an occasion in the course of a day,
beyond (the requirements of) establishing your household.
Goods will exist – follow your heart!
There's no gain in goods, when it is disaffected.

(Maxim 12)
If you are a man of excellence,
you shall beget a son for the pleasing of god.
If he is straight, he will take after your character,
and care for your goods in the proper way.
Do goodness for him: he is your son;
he is of your spirit's seed: may you not withdraw your heart
    from him!
Progeny (can) make trouble:

---

[1] The maxim alludes to judgement after death; 'landing' and 'mooring' are common images of death.

[2] i.e., if a man acts or acquires selfishly, it is his crime, for which he cannot use his position as an excuse. Truth is universal and impartial, and cannot be used as one likes, as if private property.

[3] Although the 'heart' is often concerned with ethical matters, this maxim seems to commend spontaneous pleasure.

if he stays and transgresses your advice, having defied all that
    was said,
his speech coming out with evil words,
you shall belabour him for his speech accordingly.
Oppose yourself to one hateful to them[4]
– he is one for whom opposition was ordained in the womb;
he whom they guide cannot go astray, whom they leave
    boatless cannot find a crossing.

(Maxim 13)
If you are in the court,
stand and sit according to your position,
which was ordained for you on the first day.
Do not overstep, or you will come to be opposed.
Clever is he who enters when announced,
and wide the access for him who is summoned.
The court is according to standard;
every affair is by measure.
It is god who advances position;
the jostler is not appointed.

(Maxim 17)
If you are a leader,
be calm when you hear a petitioner's speech,
Do not rebuff him from purging his body
of that which he planned to tell you.
One in distress loves to pour his heart out
more than accomplishing that for which he came.
As for him who rebuffs petitions, it is said: "Why does he reject
    it?"
Everything for which he petitioned may not come about,
(but) a good hearing is what soothes the heart.

(Maxim 18)
If you want to make friendship last
in a house you enter,
whether as lord, or brother, or friend,
in any place you enter,
beware of approaching the women!
The place where this is done cannot be good;
there can be no cleverness in revealing this.
A thousand men are turned away from their good:
a little moment, the likeness of a dream,
and death is reached by knowing them.

---

[4] 'They' are the gods: if a son turns out bad, he should be disowned, as the gods are against him. Elsewhere, Ptahhotep presents such a fate as the result of personal choice, not predestination.

It is a vile thing, conceived by an enemy;
one emerges from doing it
with a heart (already) rejecting it.
As for him who ails through lusting after them, no plan of his
   can (ever) succeed.

(Maxim 19)
If you wish your condition to be good,
protect yourself from every evil.
Beware of a selfish man's deed.
It is a painful disease of an incurable.
He who catches it cannot exist: it makes trouble with fathers
   and mothers,
and also with brothers by the same mother;
it drives apart husband and wife.
It is the sum of all evil;
it is a compound of all that is hateful.
A man shall endure when he uses Truth aright.
He who goes according to his position
makes a legacy by this: there is no tomb for the selfish.

(Maxim 21)
If you are excellent, you shall establish your household,
and love your wife according to her standard:
fill her belly, clothe her back;
perfume is a prescription for her limbs.

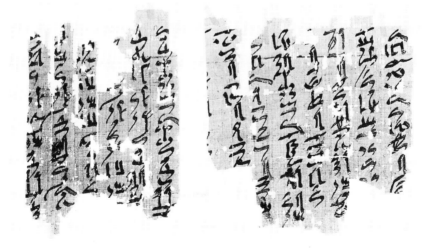

The 'Teaching of Ptahhotep', written in a fine mid-12th-Dynasty literary hand. This
manuscript comes from Thebes, and these fragments contain maxims 21 and 22
(BM 10371/10435; H. 15 cm).

Make her happy as long as you live!
She a field, good for her lord.
You shall not pass judgement on her.
Remove her from power, suppress her;
her eye when she sees (anything) is her stormwind.[5]
This is how to make her endure in your house:
you shall restrain her. A female
who is in her own hands is like the rainwater:
she is sought, and she has flown away.

(Maxim 22)
Gratify your close friends with what comes to you,
which has happened to one favoured by god.
As for him who fails to gratify his close friends,
it is said: "Isn't he a nice spirit!"
What will happen cannot be known, when thinking of
   tomorrow.
A spirit by whom people are gratified is a true spirit.
If occasions of favour come,
it is close friends who say: "Welcome",
(and if) supplies are not brought to town,
then close friends are brought, when there are difficulties.'

16 Social solidarity: from the 'Loyalist Teaching'

The full 'Loyalist Teaching' is known only from New Kingdom fragments (three papyri, a writing board and sixty-five ostraca); the funerary stela of Sehotepibre, an official of Amenemhat III, contains an edited version of the first half which urges loyalty to the king (hence the modern title). The design of his stela harks back to that of the vizier Montuhotep who succeeded Intefiqer in office under Senwosret I, and the Teaching may well come from the same reign. The name of the teacher is lost from all manuscripts, although enough survives to show that he was almost certainly a vizier.

The second half, which is given here, deals with the relationship between an official and the common people. The dependence of society on the peasants is presented in gnomic epigrams, drawing on the metaphor of men as cattle: society needs both rulers and the ruled, while the anti-social individual is doomed. In the final three stanzas this social solidarity is allied to the idea of reciprocity and retribution which is integral to the doctrine of Truth (as shown in **10, 14**), and in the very last these qualities are viewed *sub specie aeternitatis*, with imagery of burial. The explicit treatment of this topic is quite unparalleled in Middle Kingdom writings.

'You shall praise these (maxims) after years,
for their soundness is what gives landfall.
Another instance for forming your hearts
– which is better than anything – concerning your servants:

---

[5] A wife grows stormy and unsettled when she sees anything, and so should be kept under control. This is because, otherwise, a woman is like water: when she is wanted she will have gone away. These lines continue the agriculture and storm metaphors.

Provide for men, gather people together,
that you may secure(?) servants who are active.
It is men who create that which exists;
one lives on what comes from their hands.
They are lacking, and poverty prevails.

The provider of provisions is the professions.
Empty is a house, with its foundations shaken –
the (very) sound of them builds up its walls (again)!
He who sleeps until dawn is a lord of multitudes;
there shall be no sleep for the single man.
One does not send a lion on a mission.[1]
There exists no herd which can isolate itself from the enclosure;
its voice is like the thirsty animal's outside the well,
with [distress] around it, and the wailing of birds.

One (must) long for the Inundation – one profits by it;
there is no ploughed field which exists of itself.
The cattle who are with a cowherd are great:
it is the rancher who can lead the wild bull;
it is [the shepherd who ferries the animals(?)] across to land;
[The shepherded] will be a plentiful flock, without number!
This is an office excellent to god.
As for him capable of it – he's clever.
Do not make the labourer wretched with taxes;
enrich him and he will be there for you the next year.
If he lives, you are in his hands.[2]
You bring him low, and then he decides to be a fugitive.

He who appoints the taxes in proportion to the corn,
he is [a just] man in the eyes of god.
The riches of the unjust cannot stay;
his children cannot benefit from (any) remainder.
He who afflicts is making the end of his life.
There are no children of his close to him.
Serfs belong to the one who passes over himself.
There are no heirs for the violent-hearted.
Great is the reverence paid to the lord of his temperament;
the loud-voiced is unjust in (all) eyes.

It is the evil one who destroys his (own) mound,
while a town is founded for the loved one.
Patience is the monument of a man.

---

[1] Anyone who is solitary, like the proverbially sleepless lion, is excluded from social business.

[2] i.e., dependent on him.

Excellent is the silent one, [more than .....]
He who foresees what will come [has never been repulsed(?)];
the mighty of command prevails.
The merciful – the cow bears for him;
the evil shepherd – his herd is small.

Fight for men in all circumstances.
They are a flock, excellent for their lord.
It is they by whom one evidently lives;
they are also excellent in burial.
May you look to [your ....];
may you watch over your funerary priests:
recalcitrant the son, remaining the priest.
He is full of grace, the one who is called "heir".
Conduct the noble dead (to burial); make invocations in his
    name;
[honour] the blessed dead; bring offer[ings]!
[This is more excellent for] the doer than for him for whom it is
    done –
the Cared one[3] protects him who is still on earth.'

[IT IS COME, WELL AND] IN PEACE.[4]

17 The bureaucrat's view of society: from the 'Teaching of Duaf's son Khety'

The name of the author of this teaching is in doubt, as all the manuscripts are corrupt New Kingdom copies, but he is probably the same Khety who is credited as the author of the 'Teaching of Amenemhat' in **60b**. The date implied by this attribution, at the start of the 12th Dynasty when a new administration was being formed, accords well with the teaching's promotion of scribedom. Given the unreliable state of the text, the excerpts translated here draw heavily on conflations and emendations.

Khety presents his son with vignettes of non-scribal professions, suffused with a grim and scornful humour, which have led Egyptologists to call his teaching the 'Satire on Trades'. The interdependence of society advanced in the 'Loyalist Teaching' is lacking in this portrayal of the populace's baseness and of the gap between it and the literate elite. However, this gap may not have been impassable: the remarks made by the washermen's children suggest that some social advancement might have been possible. The teaching must assume that some people could choose to be literate (or else why advocate literacy?), and other texts also imply that a degree of meritocracy was accommodated within the social hierarchy. The second, shorter half of the text provides advice for the civil servant, and concludes in praise of the scribe's good fortune, in which the relationship between parents and children is acclaimed as the channel through which literacy and wisdom are passed down.

---

[3] The noble dead, for whom the rituals are done.

[4] Only part of the colophon is preserved, and only in one New Kingdom manuscript.

A model granary showing workers being supervised by a scribe with a writing-board on his knees (BM 41573; L. 36 cm).

BEGINNING OF THE TEACHING
MADE BY the man of Sile,
called Duaf's son Khety
for his son called Pepy,
while journeying south to the Residence
to place him in the scribal school,
in the midst of the children of the officials and the foremost of
  the Residence.

Then he said to him: 'I have seen beatings!
Set your heart to writings.
Observe how people are seized for labour.
Look, there is no excelling writings – they are (like) a boat on
  water.
Read at the end of "Kemit",[1]
and you will find these verses in it, saying:
"As for a scribe in any position in the Residence,
he shall not be wretched in it."

He fills another's need; shall he not end up content?
I cannot see another trade like it,
of which those verses could be said.

---

[1] 'Kemit', 'The Compendium(?)', was the name given to a literary letter used as a set text in scribal training.

I shall make you love writing more than your mother;
I shall present its beauties to you.
Now, it is greater than any trade.
There is not its like in the land.
When he was a child, he began to flourish;
he will be consulted, will be sent to do missions,
when he is not yet arrived at (the age to) wear a kilt.

I cannot see a sculptor on a mission,
nor a goldsmith being sent.
I have seen the metal-worker at his labour
at the mouth of his furnace,
his fingers like the stuff of a crocodile;
he stinks more than fish-roe.

....

And the barber is (still) shaving at evening's end.
To the town he takes himself;
to his corner he takes himself;
from street to street he takes himself
to search for people to shave.
He is vigorous with his arms to fill his belly,
like a bee which can eat (only) as it has worked.

....

And the gardener is bringing a yoke,
each of his shoulders weighted with age,
and with a great swelling on his neck,
which is festering;
he spends the morning watering the corianders,
and his supper is by the *Shaut*-plants,
having spent the midday in the orchard.
Because of his produce, it happens that he sinks down dying,
more so than (with) any other trade.

And the farmer laments more than the guinea fowl,
his voice louder than the raven's (?),
with his fingers made swollen
and with an excessive stink.
He is weary, having been assigned to the Delta,
and then he is in rags.
....

....

And the washerman washes on the shore,
and nearby is the crocodile.
"Father, I shall leave the flowing(?) water,"
say his son and daughter,
"for a trade that one can be content in,
more so than any other trade,"
while his food is mixed with shit.
There is no part of him clean,
while he puts himself amongst the skirts of a woman who is in
    her period(?);
he weeps, spending the day at the washing board.
He is told: "Dirty clothes!
Bring yourself over here," and the (river-)edge overflows with
    them.

The fowl-catcher, he is very wearied, gazing at the birds.
If the flocks of birds pass over him, then he says, "If only I had a
    net!"
God does not let this happen to him,
so that he is wearied by his state.

I will likewise tell you of the fisherman.
He is more wearied than (a man of) any other trade:
he who is a labourer in the river,
a consorter with crocodiles.
Even if the total of his reckoned (catch) comes to him,
then he is in woe:
doesn't he (then) say, "The crocodile's waiting!",
blinded by fear?
If he comes out of the flowing(?) water,
then he's as if smitten by god's might.
Look, no trade is free from a director,
except the scribe's: the director is him.

But if you know writings, it shall be well for you,
more than these trades I have shown you.
Look at them, at their wretchedness: none says to him
"A farmer, and a man".[2] Take heed!
Look at what I have done in coming south to the Residence,
look, I do it for your sake!
A day in the school-room is excellent for you;
it is for eternity, its works are (like) stone.
The workmen I have shown you hurry by,
risen early and rebellious.

---

[2] i.e., labourers are considered to be almost sub-human.

I shall tell you other things,
to teach you wisdom:
....

Speak not falsehood against your mother; it is the abomination
  of the officials.
As for a descendant who does what is excellent,
his actions are worthy of the past.
Do not take enjoyment with the troublesome;
it is bad when you are heard about (like this).
If you are sated with three loaves,
and two jars of beer have been drunk,
without ending (your) appetite – fight it!
If another is being sated, do not hang (around him);
beware of rushing to the table!

....

Look, I have placed you on the path of god,
for the Rennenet of a scribe is on his shoulder,
on the day of his birth.
He shall reach office, (as) one to whom men bow.
Look, there is no scribe lacking food,
or goods from the palace l.p.h..
Meskhenet is ordained to a scribe –
she who advances him before the council.
Thank god for your father and your mother,
who put you on the path of life.
Look at these (maxims) I have put before you
and the children of your children.'

IT IS COME, WELL AND IN PEACE.[3]

18–20 The codification and mobilisation of knowledge

18 An onomasticon

The so-called 'onomastica' are lists of nouns arranged in categories without definition or explanation. They are not merely lists for teaching vocabulary, but represent a way of classifying existence into patterns, through the power of the word. This example was found in the 13th-Dynasty 'Ramesseum library' (see **3**); the hand suggests a date late in the 12th Dynasty or at the start of the 13th. The title is lost, but was probably similar to that of a later New Kingdom onomasticon, which articulates the universal aspect of the genre very directly. This begins:

BEGINNING OF THE TEACHING OF MAKING INTELLIGENT,
  of instructing the ignorant and of knowing all that is ....

---

[3] The New Kingdom version of the colophon.

The text itself consists of a list of words, each written on a separate line, with the determinatives in a distinct sub-column; in such a way the types of articles could be recognised easily. The lines were numbered, which is unusual. At the end is a note that the number of words falls short of the total which should have been included by twenty; in fact two items were omitted beyond this. The groups and the lists are very selective – for example, that of fruit ignores figs and grapes – and the criteria for inclusion are obscure. At a later date another list of twenty types of cattle was added to the main onomasticon; its lines were unnumbered.

The items named in the main onomasticon are as follows:

1–90	[plants and liquids]
91–2	oils
93–121	plants and liquids (including some minerals and wickerwork!)
122–33	birds
134–52	fish
153–63	birds
164–70	desert animals
171–87	fortresses of Nubia and Upper Egypt
188–215	towns of Upper Egypt (in this group the sub-column of determinatives is replaced by one of abbreviations for the names)
216–53	bread, cakes and confectionery (this group has a heading 'Things placed in water', which refers to the practice of moistening bread before eating)
254–65	cereals
266–70	minerals (perhaps used as seasonings, as 'salt' is included)
271–311	anatomical parts (used in butchery)
312–23	fruits and tree-produce

The final lines (315 ff.) read:

> 'salt'-fruit (= fenugreek)
> 'natron'-fruit(?)
> unripe sycamore figs
> persea fruit
> berry of Christ-thorn
> 320 bark of *st*[...]
> aniseed
> interior of fenugreek

Total 323 (items); not 343 (as there should have been).

19 A mathematical problem

Mathematical, like medical, texts featured considerably in collections of papyri, including those from el-Lahun (see **28**). They are not analytic or theoretical treatises, but lists of practical examples for solving problems encountered in administrative and building works. The example here is problem 66 from Papyrus Rhind, which was copied in the Hyksos period from a 12th-Dynasty original, as the title states:

> THE STANDARD OF ENTERING INTO MATTERS,
> KNOWING ALL THAT IS, [ALL] THE OBSCURE THINGS,
> [ALL .....], AND ALL SECRETS.
> Now this roll was copied in Year 33, month 4 of Akhet,
> [under the Person of the Dual] King: Aawoserre, given life,
> according to the writings of old,
> made in the time of the Dual [King: Nima]atre.
> It was the scribe Ahmose who copied this document.

(Problem 66:)

FAT (WORTH) 10 GALLONS is issued for one year. What is the daily share of it? The working out: you shall make this fat (worth) 10 gallons into *ro*;[1] this makes 3200. You shall make the year into days; this makes 365. You shall divide 3200 by 365; this makes 8 + $\frac{2}{3}$ + $\frac{1}{10}$ + $\frac{1}{2190}$ (= 8.767), making in *ro*: $\frac{1}{64}$ of a gallon (= 5 *ro*) + 3 *ro* + $\frac{2}{3}$ + $\frac{1}{10}$ + $\frac{1}{2190}$. This is the daily share. THE WORKING OUT IN STAGES:

1	365
2	730
4	1460
‹8	2920›
$\frac{2}{3}$	243$\frac{1}{3}$
$\frac{1}{10}$	36$\frac{1}{2}$
$\frac{1}{2190}$	$\frac{1}{6}$ TOTAL: 8 + $\frac{2}{3}$ + $\frac{1}{10}$ + $\frac{1}{2190}$

You shall do likewise regarding all that you are told (to do), just like this example.

20 Gynaecological prescriptions

Medical texts are always obscure because of flaws in our lexicographical knowledge, which make the recipes impossible to reconstruct. These gynaecological prescriptions come from a papyrus (100 x 30 cm) from el-Lahun (see **28**); an account written on the verso is dated to 'year 38 (of Amenemhat III)'. Three long pages of horizontal lines contain thirty-four such prescriptions without any introductory title, and the roll shows evidence of having been much used. It may have come from the temple library.

The prescriptions are structured round the questioning of a patient, and the first displays the use of sympathetic magic which was an integral part of Egyptian medicine.

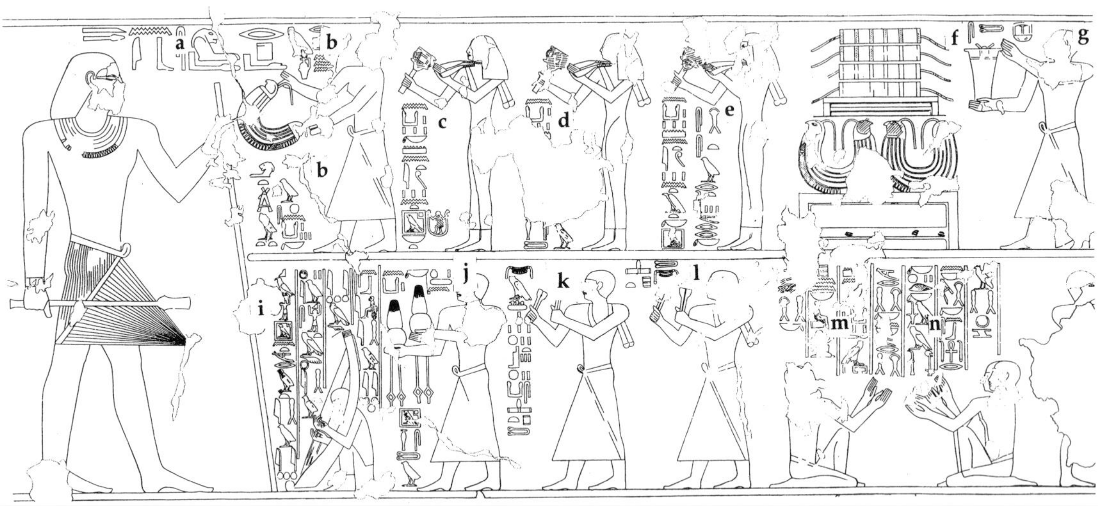

[1] A *ro* is $\frac{1}{320}$ of a gallon.

(Prescription 2)

SAFEGUARDING a woman, whose vagina is sore during movement. YOU SHALL SAY TO HER: 'What is it you smell?' If she says to you: 'I keep smelling roasting.' YOU SHALL SAY TO HER: 'It is *nemsu*-symptoms from the vagina.' YOU SHALL ACT FOR HER (thus): fumigate her with whatever she smells as roasting.

(Prescription 3)

SAFEGUARDING a woman, suffering in her backside, her pubic region and the roots of her thighs. YOU SHALL SAY TO HER: 'It is *khaau*-symptoms from the vagina.' YOU SHALL MAKE FOR HER: rootstock of *Cyperus esculentus*, **5** *ro*; valerian(?), **5** *ro*; cow milk, 1 half-litre jar; cooked, cooled and made into one substance; and drunk for four mornings.

21 A prince's court: a scene from the tomb of Sonebi

Tomb walls were often decorated with idealised scenes of the deceased feasting, watching his servants and the like, all suggestive of the prosperity he also wished to enjoy in the Netherworld. Other scenes would show his funeral and the presentation of mortuary offerings. Although these scenes are not directly taken from actual life, they are the most vivid images of it that we can hope to have.

The provincial governor of the 14th Upper Egyptian Nome under Amenemhat I and Senwosret I, Ukhhotep's son Sonebi, was buried in a fine tomb at Meir. On the north wall of the rock-cut chapel is the following scene (H. 73 cm), showing a ceremony performed in his honour. He is presented with ceremonial collars, and menats (necklaces) and sistra (rattles) sacred to Hathor, goddess of love and rebirth. A harpist sings, while ritual bread is offered and castanets played. Other figures dance as they extol Sonebi and wrestle. Each figure is

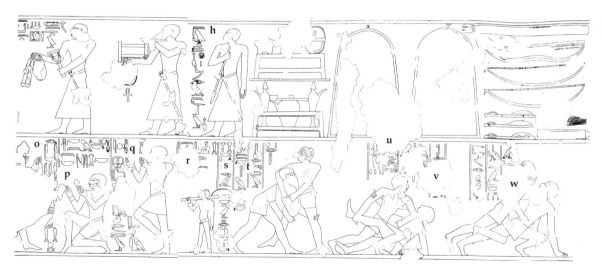

A ceremony in honour of Count Sonebi (H. 73 cm; from *Meir* I, pl.2–3).

accompanied by a caption giving his name or recording his speech; most are eulogies or lyrics from the ceremony, but the wrestlers are sarcastically taunting each other.

(a)   The Patrician and Count
       Sonebi, true of voice.

(b) (to Sonebi)   The steward Khnum:
       The first of the adornment: a collar for your spirits!

(c)   For your spirits!
       Menats of Hathor, lady of Cusae!

(d)   For your spirits!
       [Menats of Hathor] – may she favour you!

(e)   For ‹your› spirits!
       Menats of your mother Hathor
       – may she make you last for as many years as you wish!

(f)   Oil.

(g)   For your spirit‹s›!
       Menats of Hathor – may she favour you!

(h) (to Hathor)   May you pass by(?)! Fair is the day; may it
       see happiness!

(i)   Exalted is Hathor, she of love!
       O castanets! castanets!
       She is exalted, on (this) free day!
       O castanets!
       On (this) free (day), O Sonebi!
       O castanets!

(j)   For your spirit!
       An offering-loaf of Hathor's – may she favour you!

(k)   O Gold in the pools, the pools,
       the places, the places of her spirit! May you be
       gracious!

(l)   May you be gracious, O Gold!

(m)   How the spirits stay here, in this house!
       My lord, I wish you to live long!

(n)   I wish you to live long, my lord!
       I wish you to live long, to live long!
       May you pass a thousand years!
       I wish you to live long,
       healthily and alive, for eternity![1]

(o)   May you make favour [.. ....] for eternity!

(p)   As you live for me,[2] look, a happy day!
       My lord, I wish you to live long!

(q)   May you repeat a million jubilees! May Hathor kiss
       you in them!

---

[1] (m) and (n) chant together, clapping their hands.

[2] A formulaic oath.

(r)   O Sonebi, enduring of name!

(s) (to t)   Please be patient! and you'll see yourself on your face!

(t) (to s)   I'll bring you that! Look, I make you fall on it (your face)!

(u–v)   (Too broken to be understood)

(w)   Don't boast! Look how we're here! Look at you!

22–4 Scenes of low life from various tombs

These scenes of low life are no less idealised than the preceding scene: the most frequent remark is an obedient 'All right' (literally 'I shall do as you favour')! The workmen's phrases are standardised, following traditions established in the Old Kingdom, and the language is not truly colloquial, although less formal than in tomb texts such as autobiographies (metre was not appropriate for all the captions). Nevertheless, in some there is a strong sense of humour, character and spontaneity.

22 Baking and brewing

This scene (H. 100 cm) comes from the Theban rock-cut tomb of Senet, the mother of the vizier Intefiqer who served under the first two kings of the 12th Dynasty; he is well known from various documents (see **27**). It is part of the north wall of the passage leading to the offering chamber. In it two men are shown grinding grain with pestle and mortar. Next the grain is ground with a quern and sieved by two women, one of whom piously prays for her

Baking and brewing scenes (H. 100 cm; from Davies-Gardiner, *Antefoqer*, pl.11).

master, while her companion replies more cynically. The dough is then baked in moulds. In the lower register beer is being prepared from dough: it is kneaded together with dates, then mixed with water (despite a child's interruptions). Finally it is poured into jars to ferment:

(a) (to b) Down!
(b)   All right!
(c)   O all gods of this land, make my strong master healthy!
(d) (to c) [.....] Look, this is for (my own) food!
(e) (to c) All right!
            Look, this is green firewood! Look, I'd better be thanked!
(f)   These dates from the store are old.
            If only I'd seen them when they were first issued! Then I could've done some good!
(g) (to h) Give me some fermented lees,[1] look, I'm hungry!
(h) (to g) May you, and she who bore you, be driven off by a hippopotamus
            – you eat more than a royal slave at the plough!
            Look, you're stopping [me from] work!

23 Harvesting flax

This scene is from the north wall of the tomb of Sonebi (see **21**, which adjoins this). It shows two men squabbling while they harvest flax (H. 38 cm).

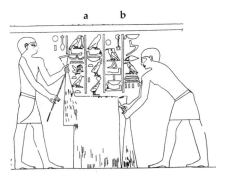

Flax-harvesting (H. 38 cm; from *Meir* I, pl.3).

(a) Look, you're (just) pulling, without picking. And the day is good (for work)!
(b) Look to your own arm and then give a glance at us!

---

[1] *Sermet*, the solid remains of the dough.

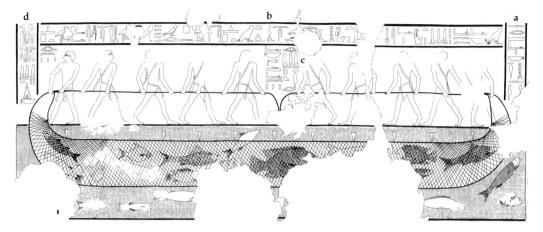

Fishing with a net (H. 85 cm; from *El-Bersheh* I, pl.22).

24 Fishing

This scene of fishing (H. 85 cm) is on the rear wall of the offering chamber of the tomb of Djehutihotep, who governed the 15th Upper Egyptian nome under Senwosret II and III. His funerary complex was particularly grand, including a colossal statue as well as the tomb cut into the cliffs at el-Bersha (see also **39f**). Here the men are told to sing a work song (a), which is recorded along the top of the scene (b).

(a) Stretch out your arm and sing!
(b) Look, Sokhet gives us her hand.
Good is Sokhet; she has caught a 'Welcome!'
for this Friend, the Greatest of the Five in the Temple of
Thoth,
whom she loves and praises,
the Count Djehutihotep!
(c) Work, excellent peasant, and let us make a catch!
(d) [.....] peasant, and let us work!

25 A bucolic fantasy: from 'The Pleasures of Fishing and Fowling'

The late 18th-Dynasty papyrus, which is the sole copy of the so-called 'Pleasures of Fishing and Fowling', is very fragmentary and prevents a full understanding of the literary structure. However, it seems to be a monologue by a man on a hunting expedition into the marshes with his lord, which describes and eulogises the type of bucolic trip so often represented on tomb walls (see illustration on p. 84). Internal evidence suggests a date of composition in the late 12th Dynasty. In these two stanzas the speaker, who is presumably now a town-dwelling official, addresses his lord and gives voice to a pastoral longing for the rustic life; a more immediate description of netting fowl follows.

'Would that I were (always) in [the country],
[that I might do] the things that my heart desired,
as when the countryside was my town,

Hunting in the marshes from the tomb of Count Sonebi (H. 73 cm; from *Meir* I, pl. 2).
This is immediately below **21**. The captions read:
    'Spearing fish by the blessed one
    before Osiris, lord of the western necropolis,
    the Count and Overseer of Priests,
    Sonebi, true of voice'
    and
    'Casting the throw stick at birds
    by the Count, the Royal Seal-bearer, the Sole Friend,
    Sonebi, true of voice'
He is accompanied by
    'his wife and favourite,
    Meres, possessor of blessedness'.

and the head of the meadow was [my dwelling place – which I
    have not (since) seen(?)],
[that I were with] the people my heart desired and with friends,
and that I might spend the day in the place of my longing,
[in the .....(?) and in] the papyrus clumps.
At dawn, I would have a bite,
and be far away, walking in the place of my heart.

I would walk [along] the river,
on the second and fifteenth day feasts,
and go down to the pool,
with the staves upon my arm's shoulder,
my poles at my back(?),
the two and a half cubits (of rope) in my armpit,
and my attention (given) to tugging the draw rope in my hand.
(Now) the water shall be stirred(?), and the (signal)-cloth[1]
held by the hand shall be at the pool,
as we see it fall, having heard the cries of its fowl.
We shall snare them in the net;
the bush and the [....] of [...]
[become a feasting place(?)] for us, for six hours.
The end is come, come to pass as your carefreeness.'

---

[1] A cloth waved to tell the men when to pull the clapnet shut.

26 A royal decree

This is the second of two decrees which were inserted into a Theban administrative document (33) in use from the late 12th to the mid-13th Dynasty; it was jotted down on a blank area of the register, upside down (see illustration on p. 100). Both decrees and the main text on the roll concern labourers; this decree resulted from a local official's having appealed to the king, probably Amenemhat-Sobekhotep (II), about the labourers who had been assigned to him from the 'Office of (enforced) Labour', but who were then reassigned to another estate. His request for replacements was heard and a representative of the king sent this decree to the vizier with instructions to be passed to the Theban authorities. It seems that the vizier Ankhu, who is known from other sources and who probably served under both Amenemhat-Sobekhotep (II) and Khendjer, sent a copy of the decree to Thebes where it was entered into the records thus:

Year 6, month 3 of Peret, day 3:
(COPY OF) ANOTHER ROYAL DECREE BROUGHT TO THE OFFICE OF THE REPORTER OF THE SOUTHERN CITY.
A Royal Decree to the Lord Vizier, the Overseer of the 6 Great mansions, Ankhu: Look, this decree of the king is brought to you to inform you that the Treasurer of the King, the Overseer of Fields of the Southern City, [Hauankhu's son Ib]ia, has made petition, saying: 'The field labourers in my estate, from the "Labour Office" of the Residence, are taken away from Iatsekhetiu,[1] (though) they were given to me from the "Office of Labour". Redeem me, my lord, letting me be given (people) in exchange (for them)!' – so he said. Look, what has been done is heard. Look what is ordered to the appropriate authority who is in the Residence: 'You shall have directives issued for the appropriate authorities who are in the Southern City!' May you act accordingly. Look, the king l.p.h. is safe and sound! (May) your heart be likewise!

27 Accounts of a royal dockyard workshop at Thinis

When the anonymous tomb 408 at Nag' el-Deir was excavated, four papyri were found rolled up on top of one of the wooden sarcophagi. It is uncertain why they were placed in the tomb; it is unlikely that they were left there by accident or were the work of the actual tomb owner taken into the next life. Perhaps he was a scribe and they were placed there as a symbol of his professional status. The second of these provincial administrative documents was once 33 × 230 cm and contained the accounts of a royal dockyard workshop under Senwosret I at nearby Thinis, with registers of equipment spanning more than three years. The intense detail of the records kept suggests a high level of supervision in the administration.

The part translated here covers month 2 of Akhet in year 17 of Senwosret I (1901 BC). During this period two orders arrived from the vizier in the capital and were copied into the register with a note of who had delivered them. The first contained instructions about the collection of a load of an unknown substance (*Argemti*), and the second, which arrived the next day, contained the vizier's afterthoughts: the stewards must also deliver some cereals to the capital, and must be sure to impress his agent with a proper welcome. The vizier Intefiqer is well known: he served Amenemhat I and Senwosret I for at least thirty years; he constructed a mastaba in the pyramid enclosure of the first king, and then, apparently, a larger one in that of Senwosret. This latter shows possible signs of deliberate destruction, as

[1] A place name, meaning 'The-mound-of-peasants'.

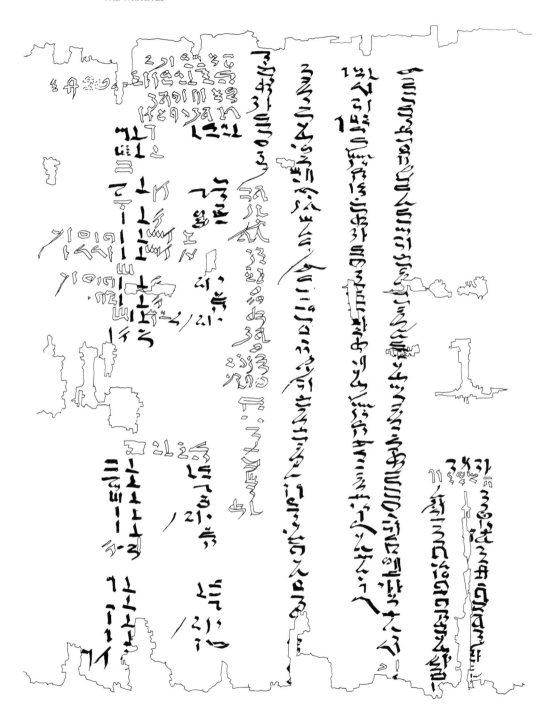

Papyrus Reisner II: the second letter from Intefiqer and the accounts (H. 33 cm; red ink is represented by hollow lines).

does the rock-cut tomb of his mother Senet at Thebes (see **22, 47, 59**). One of his two known sons, Intefiqer and Wen, was cursed in a later execration text (**46**), which suggests that he had rebelled and brought dishonour on his father. His wife was called Satsasobek.

The account is a register of copper tools delivered to the workshop, which are listed by type, weight and number. A second register summarises the first, omitting a short-weight tool (the unidentified *Teha*).

Year 17, MONTH 2 OF AKHET, DAY 7:
The Lord Vizier, Overseer of the 6 Great Mansions, Intefiqer.
A command to the stewards: Montuwoser's son Montuwoser[1]
                  Rudi's son Sobekankh
                  Henu's son Intef
                  Djebas' son Dedu's son Dedu[1]
                  Iy's son Inherhotep
                  Nakhti's son Ankeku
                  Intef's son Senankhu:
[... ... ...] furnish equipment from [you]r equipment! Each one of you shall be at his landing place: be prepared! I am the one writing about the cargo, and it is each one of you who shall take the paddles and the trestles in his own boat, without letting (them) go down [into the water(?). ....]; also get ready(?) the *Argemti*, about which I have written to you – the choicest of the choice belongs to your store! Now you shall do (this) until the vizier's scribe Nakht finds your store of *Argemti* (ready) upon the bank. Look, I've caused him to come about loading it; also get me 30 men for the crew of the boats, each one of them strong.
BROUGHT BY THE OFFICIAL AND DIGNITARY, MASU'S SON INTEF, THE CREW OF SAAGRETEB.[2]

Year 17,
MONTH 2 OF AKHET, DAY 8:
The Lord Vizier, Overseer of the 6 Great mansions, Intefiqer.
A command to the Overseers of the Great House, who are in the Thinite nome. Make sure you have yourselves shaved and get yourselves ready just as I laid down for you; also have sent downstream **150** gallons of wheat, [with] a double gallon of malt, and 10,000 *Ter*-loaves, to the Residence – each one of you! Look, I shall take account of it at the Residence, for getting this wheat as new wheat is a (critical) matter – it must be attained. Have him shaved and provide a serving girl of the Storehouse, a strong one [... ...] for each one of you from him.
BROUGHT BY THE OFFICIAL AND DIGNITARY MONTUHOTEP'S SON MONTUHOTEP,[1] AND INTEF'S SON MONTUHOTEP'S SON SONBEF OF THE CREW OF SAAGRETEB.[2]

[1] Written simply 'M's son, ditto'.

[2] The name – a rather unusual one – of the head of the crew to which the messenger belonged.

MONTH 2 OF AKHET, DAY 22:
ACCOUNT OF COPPER GIVEN TO THE DOCKYARD WORKSHOP:
FOREMAN ISI'S SON INTEF
SCRIBE INTEF'S SON SEFKHY:

		weights of copper		units	
Copper:	axes	50	copper:	5	
		40	copper:	3	
			(=) 8		
	adzes	15	copper:	7	
			(=) 7		
	chisels	20	copper:	1	
		14	copper:	1 OUTWORKER NEBIT	
		14	copper:	1 IKEKI	
			(=) 3		
	Teha	20	copper:	1 OUTWORKER NEBIT	
	gravers	20	copper:	1 [...]	
	small *Teha*	SHORT-WEIGHT	copper:	1 (=) 3	
			Total: 21		

ACCOUNT OF COPPER:

axes	copper:	8	
adzes	copper:	7	
chisels	copper:	3	
Teha	copper:	1	
gravers	copper:	1	
	Total:	**20**	

28 From the temple archive at el-Lahun

These and the following documents are from in el-Lahun, the town founded by Senwosret II in connection with his cult at the neighbouring pyramid complex which was called 'Power-of-Senwosret-true-of-voice'. The town was called 'Peace-of-Senwosret-true-of-voice'. It was laid out on a rectangular plan, some 384 × 335 m, with the accommodation sharply divided into groups of large houses for the elite and small houses for others, in a ratio 1:20. The population has been estimated at 3,000. One temple in the town was dedicated to Sopdu, Lord of the East, although the royal funerary cult provided another major focus of religious activity, and apparently was dedicated to Anubis. The community was administered by the 'count' (the mayor), and by the vizier on his occasional visits. The heterogeneous group of el-Lahun papyri covers the second half of the 12th Dynasty and the start of the 13th, and does not represent a single archive but a conflation of several. The collection, still not fully published, is now divided between London and Berlin (with additional fragments in Cairo). Many of the documents are administrative letters and records (**29, 36–8**) which are probably from at least two official archives (see **29c**). This first selection, however, is from the archive of the funerary temple (as are probably **7, 20, 42**); this contained, as well as a library, a typical range of accounts, inventories of equipment, lists of personnel and the like.

28a is one of the reports entered into the temple daybook when the band of priests on duty for the month (the 'phyle') was changed.

28b–c are letters copied into the daybook, and refer explicitly to this practice; presumably other less relevant letters were simply read and discarded. The first is crucial to the chronology of the period, as it gives the date of the heliacal rising of the Dog-star Sothis, so that the priests could plan the appropriate ceremonies for the correct day. The letter is dated, as is usual, simply 'Year 7, month 3 of Peret, day 25,' without mentioning the king, who was probably Senwosret III; a Count Nubkaure, who is mentioned in a royal stela erected in year 8 of Senwosret III (BM 852), may be identical with the writer of this letter.

28c concerns the issue of an ox-hide; after the letter the copyist added a note that the hide was actually issued from the temple stores.

28a The monthly report

REPORT OF THE FOURTH PHYLE OF THE TEMPLE PRIESTHOOD WHO ARE WITHDRAWING FOR THE MONTH.

THIS IS THEIR STATEMENT: 'All your affairs are safe and sound. We have examined all the goods of the temple and everything of the temple is safe and sound for the first phyle of the temple priesthood who are entering for the month.'

REPORT OF THE FIRST PHYLE OF THE TEMPLE PRIESTHOOD WHO ARE ENTERING FOR THE MONTH.

THIS IS THEIR STATEMENT: 'All your affairs are safe and sound. We have received all the goods of the temple safe and sound from the fourth phyle of the temple priesthood, who were withdrawing for the month. The temple is flourishing with all goodness.'

28b The star rising

The Count, Overseer of the Temple Nubkaure, says to the Lector-priest and Chief Pepyhotep: 'a statement that you should know that the Coming Forth of Sothis will happen on month 4 of Peret, day 16. Let this be noted [by] the temple priesthood of Power-of-Senwosret-true-of-voice, of Anubis who is upon his mountain, and of Sobek; also cause this letter to be entered in the temple daybook.'

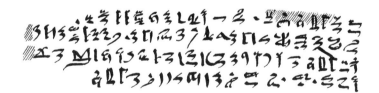

The letter, recording the Sothic rising (L. 15 cm; adapted from Möller, *Hier. Lesestücke* I, 19).

28c An order for an ox-hide

COPY OF A [REPORT(?) BROUGHT] FROM Peace-of-Senwosret-true-of-voice, WHICH THE SANDAL-MAKER SANKHPTAH'S SON WERENIPTAH BROUGHT:

Cause an ox-hide or a goat-hide to be brought. May you give it to Wereniptah. Also, enter it in writing.

An ox-hide, given to this sandal-maker.

29 Business letters from el-Lahun

The presence of model letters at el-Lahun testifies to the importance of professional letter-writing in the scribe's occupation. As opposed to decrees from king or vizier (e.g., **26–7**), such officials' letters began with elaborate greeting formulae, which varied according to the difference in rank between sender and recipient. Thus, a person writing to a superior (as in **29b–d**) reassures him that all is well with his goods, refers to himself as 'this humble servant' and the recipient as 'the lord l.p.h.'. The letter would conclude similarly, and invoke a good hearing for the message. These formulae are often longer than the actual message, but were meaningful in reaffirming the *status quo*. Examples of the formulae appropriate for equals and members of one family are found in **28b**, **34** and **55–7**. The methods of writing vary, but generally the letters were in horizontal lines, going on to the back of the sheet if necessary. The sheet was then folded several times vertically and once (or twice) horizontally to produce an oblong package. The name of the sender and recipient were then written on the outside in a suitable manner (compare **29b** and **34** for differing conventions), and the letter was secured by a piece of string which was wrapped around one end of the package and fastened with a clay seal.

29a A note of request

This is a terse practical note without any formulae (21 × 9 cm), similar to the copied letter of **28a**. Traces of additional signs along the left edge suggest that this sheet was cut out of an already used roll, or that it is a copy of the message kept by the sender. This would explain the placing of the sender's name at the end: it generally comes first in actual letters. The note dates to the reign of Amenemhat III (see **29c**).

> Year 4, month 4 of Shemu, day 13.
>
> Let an ox-hide be brought in good condition. Look, it's for its proper purpose – look, I've caused the sandal-maker Hotepi to come for it. Please give to him.
>
> Scribe of the Temple Horemsaf.

29b A letter of reminder

The underling Neni writes to his superior, the steward, decorously reminding him to deal with some property. Two previous letters have not produced any response. A man called Wah is known from a will (**36**) and may be the same man as the property owner mentioned here; if so, this letter may date to the early years of Amenemhat IV. The sheet is 30 × 19 cm.

> (Address:) The lord l.p.h., the Steward Iyib l.p.h.;
> from Neni.
>
> The servant of the estate, Neni, says to the Steward Iyib l.p.h.: 'This is a communication to the lord l.p.h., that all the affairs of the lord l.p.h. are safe and sound in all their places, in the favour of Sopdu, Lord of East, together with his ennead, and all the gods; even as this humble servant desires. This is a communication to the lord l.p.h. about letting attention be paid to the house of Wah, like my communication to you about it. For it is you who does everything good: (thus) shall you furnish your goodness. Look, the Overseer of the Temple Teti said to me: "Look, I have sent a communication about it to him, as well" – so he said. So, may one act accordingly, that the spirit

A letter of reminder with the address
(30 × 19 cm; from Möller, *Hier. Lesestücke* I,
19 B) and a reconstruction of the letter before
being opened.

of the Ruler[1] shall favour you. This is a communication about it.
It is a communication to the lord l.p.h. May the hearing by the
lord l.p.h. be good.'

29c A letter of appeal

This letter (33 × 29 cm) is torn away at the top two corners and along the bottom. The
restorations and interpretation are very tentative.

  The steward to whom Imbu writes is probably Horemsaf, who was mentioned in **29a**; that
letter was written before his promotion from the office of temple scribe, while this one is
from the last decade of Amenemhat III's reign. It has been suggested that the Berlin
collection of el-Lahun letters (from which these two are taken) was a single archive from the
steward's office under Amenemhat III. Imbu had previously written to the steward to tell
him that he was unable to complete a commission on which he had been sent; the steward
replied with a letter of complaint (probably to Imbu's superiors rather than directly). In this
letter Imbu protests his innocence and loyalty: he suspects that the complaint has been
stirred up by a junior servant ('the little one') complaining of neglect. Imbu denies this and
accuses the junior of malice. He urges the steward to recognise this, refers the matter to the
'official' (probably the local nomarch) who he is sure will vindicate him, and protests that his
loyalty will remain despite the accusation. After an appeal to public opinion, the letter ends
with conventional wishes for a reply.

(Address:) The lord l.p.h.;
           from Imbu.
[The servant of the estate I]mbu says: 'This is a communication
to the lord l.p.h., to say [that] all the people of the lord [l.p.h.
are sa]fe [and sound in their places, in the favour] of the Dual
King: [Kha]kheper[re, true of voice,[1] even as] this your humble
servant desires. This is a communication to the lord l.p.h. that
this humble servant said, "The lord l.p.h. has directed(?) [this
humble servant to the place] where this humble servant is, in
vain." And then the lord l.p.h. caused a letter to be sent [in
which the lord l.p.h.] asked about what the funerary priest
there[2] was doing. Is the lord l.p.h. seeking for something to do
against this humble servant? [What is it that will be done(?)]
against this humble servant? Am I not in pain, lord l.p.h.? I am
your liegeman! What is it,[lord l.p.h., what is it(?)] that will be
done against this humble servant? This humble servant has not
been told what he has done (wrong). Do not say, "An enem[y
of yours has appealed against you;" would I be(?)] your
liegeman, having turned a blind eye to the little one of the lord
l.p.h., who has appealed against me? I am not [someone who
does such things(?); but the little one of] the lord l.p.h. has
acted against what he should do. The official will say: "He has
done these things [against him(?)," and this humble servant]
will find the letter like a serpent.[3] But if, when the same

---

[1] The dead Senwosret II, patron of the town.

[2] i.e., Imbu.

[official] has been gracious to me, [all is well(?), then this humble servant will] offer up things on your happy day. May you not fight against [this humble servant who has done no wrong in] the whole [situation]. Look, people say: ["Why should he act against him?"(?)] Concerning me, you have begun to do something [of which no one approves(?) in Peace-of-Senwosret]-true-of-voice. Let a reply to this letter be sent to me, [… … …] him, and let this humble servant be sent to about (your) life, prosperity and health. This is a communication to the lord [l.p.h. May the hearing by the lord l.p.h. be good!]'

29d Hate-mail

This small sheet of papyrus (17 × 9 cm), from el-Lahun, is covered with black and red ink; two different hands have been detected, but, given the homogeneity of the content, the alteration in the hand may be the result of one scribe changing pens. If so, we have a single letter which is an angry parody of the usual formulae, and whose venom is intensified by the choice of the ill-omened colour red.[4] It is written by an official, Pepy, who is enraged at the return of a superior to el-Lahun. There is no address, and no sign that the letter was ever folded for sending.

A communication about what was said to this humble servant: 'the lord l.p.h. has arrived at Power-of-Senwosret-true-of-voice on month 4 of Shemu, day 10': how evil it is that you've come safe and sound!

MAY YOUR SPEAKING BE WITH ALL EVIL, IN THE FAVOUR OF SOBEK, LORD OF [….], WHO SHALL GIVE YOU TO HEWING, IN THE FAVOUR OF HIS SPIRIT. THE SPIRIT OF THE OVERSEER OF THE TEMPLE OF THE RULER,[5] PEPY HAS ACTED AGAINST YOU – ENDURINGLY, LASTINGLY, FOR ALL TIME AND ETERNITY. BAD BE YOUR HEARING – MAY YOU BE SMITTEN! COME TO ME AND I'LL SEE YOU – WE'LL HAVE AN EVIL TIME.

30 A report from a frontier garrison: from the 'Semna Despatches'

One of the magical papyri found in the 'Ramesseum library' (see **3**, p. 29) was written on the back of a fragmentary set of copies of administrative reports (H. 17 cm and L. at least 111 cm originally). These are reports from the southern fortress of Semna (see **6**), which detail the movements of Nubians in the vicinity and check the legality of their trading. The forts would also have checked fugitives from Egypt, escaping labour-duty (see **33, 39c**). Fragments of similar reports have been found at other Nubian fortresses from the late 12th Dynasty, and the very fact that copies of such detailed reports were kept at Thebes also testifies to the pervasiveness of the State administration. By the handwriting, the copies date to the late 12th Dynasty, and by internal evidence the reports themselves to Amenemhat III; this is the fourth of the surviving despatches.

---

[3] Apparently meaning that the steward's hurtful letter of complaint will slip away like a snake from Imbu's memory when it is realised that the misdeed is the junior's. Imbu will then be suitably grateful.

[4] If there are two hands, the papyrus contains a note by an unnamed scribe, and an equally ironic reply by Pepy.

[5] i.e., of the dead Senwosret II.

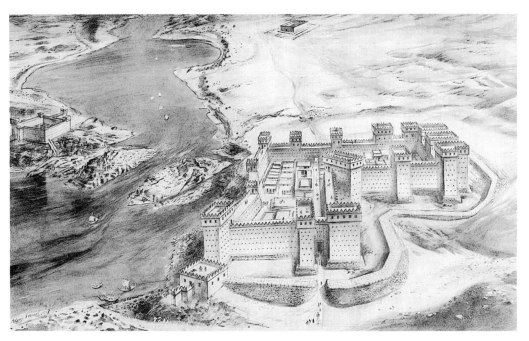

The fortress of Semna; a reconstruction by A. Sorrell.

ANOTHER LETTER BROUGHT TO HIM[1] FROM THE LIEGEMAN AMENY
WHO IS AT KHESEF-MEDJAIU,[2] being (a message) sent by fortress
to fortress: This is a communication to the lord l.p.h., that the
soldier from Nekhen, Senu's son Heru's son Reniqer, and the
soldier fromTjebu, Rensi's son Senwosret's son Senwosret,[3]
came to report to this humble servant on year 3, month 4 of
Peret, day 2, at the time of breakfast, on a mission from the
officer of the town regiment, Khusobek's son Montuhotep's
son Khusobek [....], who is deputy to the office of the Ruler's
crew in the garrison of Meha,[4] saying: 'The patrol that went out
to patrol the desert edge [right up to(?)] the fortress of Khesef-
Medjaiu on year 3, month 3 of Peret, last day, has returned to
report to me, saying, "We found the track of thirty-two men
and three donkeys, which they trod [...............]" [...] the
patrol [...] my places' – so [he said.........] order(?) of the
garrison [..........] on the desert edge. This humble servant has

[1] The unnamed recipient of the despatches, a high-ranking officer at Semna.

[2] 'Repeller of the Medjai people', the name of a fortress further north at Serra East.

[3] Written 'Rensi's son, Senwosret's son, ditto'.

[4] A district of Nubia, perhaps in the area of Abu-Simbel.

sent [about it to Semna as (a message) sent by fortress to] fortress. It is a communication [about] it. [All the affairs of the king's domain] l.p.h. are safe [and sound].

31 Three graffiti from campaigns to Nubia

At Gebel el-Girgawi, some 180 km south of Elephantine, there were over seventy crude rock-cut inscriptions, now flooded by Lake Nasser. No trace of a permanent fortress was found in the area, but there was probably a temporary encampment (the 'enclosure' of **31b**) for a series of military campaigns under Amenemhat I and Senwosret I, participation in which the graffiti commemorate. Two seal-bearers of the king record being sent on expeditions against the Nubian kingdom of Wawat over a period of twenty years. These campaigns resulted in a chain of fortresses, including Buhen, which were later expanded by Senwosret III (see **6, 30**). The incised graffiti vary in quality, and the texts' style points clearly to funerary stelae and autobiographies as models (e.g., compare **31b** with the narrative section of **53**); all are difficult to read. The three translated here are from the reign of Senwosret I.

31a (29 × 29 cm) is six lines very crudely incised on a boulder.

31b is more elaborate and careful (48 × 70 cm). It forms an oblong stela on the rock-face, with a border, a crude figure of Intefiqer, and an autobiographical account of his activity. It is almost certainly from year 29 of Amenemhat I. At the end the scribe who cut the text for him added his own record and name, which spilled over on to the border. The comparatively careful execution of the stela suggests that Intefiqer called Gem might even be the same Intefiqer as the well-known vizier mentioned by the scribe (see **27**). This is one of the earliest references to the vizier.

31c (23 × 23 cm) is on a boulder, in a row of similar graffiti, 200 m downstream from **31a**; the text is around a very crude figure, with a further line scratched along the top.

31a

> Ibes' son Id's son Ibes
> at(?) the estate of [.....] Dedukhnum:
> the army came [to Wawat], which I went round
> in year 6, [month 1(?)] of Peret.
> With the army I travelled downstream.
> There was no fighting; I shall not bring a Nubian back (as
>   captive) from the land of the Nubians.

31b

> Intefiqer, who is called Gem,
> says: 'I am a valiant citizen, a pleasant man from Luxor,
> a scribe of excellent fingers,
> one who is humble, high in love for his Person,
> who [gives out] clothes among his troops.
> I speak well in the midst of people,
> a possessor of respect among his friends.
> This enclosure was being built,
> then I slaughtered Nubians and all the rest of Wawat.
> Then I went upstream in victory,
> slaughtering the Nubian in his (own) land,
> and came back downstream stripping crops,
> and cutting down the rest of their trees

so that I could put fire to their homes,
as is done against a rebel against the king.
I have not heard of another trooper doing the like.'

Reniqer says: [1] 'I made this (graffito)
while I was here with the Patrician and Count,
the Lord Vizier,
Overseer of the 6 Great Mansions, Intefiqer,
in the (ship called) "Great Oar", brought (here) by the Dual
    King: Sehotepibre,
may he live for all time, for the [...] City(?).'[2]
The scribe Reniqer,
born of Heqet, true of voice.

31c

Year 16: Iay's son
Montuwoser's son Ameny:
I am a man of the troops,
who attacks the hero, (but) who loves life and hates death.
[3] As for him who shall erase (this graffito), death shall be found
    for him.

The graffito of Ameny
(H. 23 cm).

[1] Here the text starts on the border.

[2] Perhaps a reference to Thebes?

[3] Written along the top.

32 Commemorating a mining expedition

This tall narrow stela (265 × 67 cm) was erected in year 6 of Amenemhat III at Serabit el-Khadim in Sinai. It was placed along the approach of a modest temple which had been built around a small sacred cave. This sanctuary, which was shortly to be expanded, was dedicated to Hathor, the patroness of the area and of the mining expeditions which worked the mountains. The front of the stela faced eastward into the temple and, having been exposed to wind-blown sand, is now all but completely lost. It showed the king worshipping Hathor, with the expedition leader Horurre worshipping the king. Horurre is known to have dedicated an altar the previous year in the sacred cave, and also left two other small stelae. On the back, which would have been visible to people as they entered the temple, he carved a memorial in his own name: an inscription addressed to other miners, describing his success despite the weather. The first half of the text has an uncommon motif – the doubt and opposition an official can face – which is dispelled by a reference to the king's might. Beneath these twenty-six lines are two registers (b–c) containing figures of ten important members of the expedition, and beneath them a name-list of other members (d). A continuation of this name-list was inserted on one side of the stela beneath a string of Horurre's titles.

> (East Face)
> Year 6 under the Person
> of [........]

This headed an emblematic scene showing the king with Hathor, under which were bands of titles and epithets. Of these there are two surviving traces. The first seems to acclaim the king as

> [.....] lord of joy [.....]

The second concerns Horurre:

> [.....] the Overseer of the Chamber [.....]

At the bottom was a scene of the official making offerings to the king.

> (West Face)
> (a)
> The Person of this god's sending
> the God's Seal-bearer, Overseer of the Chamber,
> the Director of Gangs, Horurre to this mining region.
> Arrival at this land in month 3 of Peret,
> when it was not the proper season for coming to this mining
> region.
>
> This God's Seal-bearer speaks before the officials who shall
> come
> to this mining region at this time: 'May you not be downcast at it!
> Look, Hathor will turn it to good luck(?).
> Observe me! I myself have done the same.
> My coming from Egypt, downcast.
> Finding the colour[1] seemed difficult to me,
> while the hill-country was hot in summer,
> the mountains were scorching and skins were troubled.

---

[1] The colour of turquoise, for which it was prized, was believed to deteriorate in certain conditions. Thus in hot weather it was feared '(good) colour' would be hard to find; the workers state Horurre's fear more strongly.

At dawn, my rally at Rakhet;[2]
and I was addressing the craftsmen about this: "Prized is he
who is in this mining region!"
And so then they said: "Turquoise is in the mountain for
   eternity;
it is the colour which has to be sought at this time.
We have heard the like before:
the mineral comes at this time,
but it is the colour which is lacking
at this painful time of summer."
And so I set out to this mining region
with the power of the king sustaining me.

Then I arrived at this land,
and I began work successfully.
My expedition arrived, fully complete.
No loss to it ever occurred; I was not downcast when faced with
   the work.
I attained the achievement of a good beginning.
I stopped (work) on the first of Shemu, having acquired this
   precious stone.
I did more than any who had come (before), than any
   (previous) weight.
There was no "O for good colour,"[3] and eyes were in festival.
She was better than at her proper times.
Offer, offer to the Lady of Heaven!
May you propitiate Hathor!
May you do this, it is good for you!
Increase this, and it is well with you!
Very well did I make my expedition.
There were no raised voices against my labour,
and what I did was successful,
the whole expedition of young men remained [....]
[...............]
[...............]'

(b)
[...........]
[...........]
[...........]
[...........]
The Keeper of the Chamber, Ibu

[2] An unknown place, apparently on the route to the mining region in Sinai.

[3] i.e., there were no complaints about a lack of the desired 'colour'.

(c)
The Keeper of the Chamber, Khnumnakht
The Keeper of the Chamber, Ukem
The Keeper of the Chamber of the Treasury, Renefsoneb
The domestic servant and quarryman,[4] Khentyhotep
The scorpion magician,[5] Inpunakht

(d)
Expedition Overseer of Stonecutters, Khet
The quarryman of malachite, Kemen
The quarryman of malachite, Sobeku
The quarryman of malachite, Hori
The quarryman, Ik
The quarryman, Seshen
The quarryman, Khenibeb
The quarryman, Ipu
The Cup-bearer, Netjeriref
The priest, Gebu
The quarryman, Ii
The stonecutter, Sebekemesh

(Sides:)
The true Royal Acquaintance, whom he loves, his favourite,
the Friend of the Great House, the God's Seal-bearer,
Horurre, true of voice
[begotten of(?)] Sobekaa.
(Incised below this on the north side are more members of the expedition:)
The stonecarver, Sa[..]neb,
conceived of Nutmes
The stonecutter, Khentikhetihotep
The domestic servant of the Treasury, Ip
The Cup-bearer, Ini,
The Cup-bearer, Ta[…]r

33 A register of forced-labour fugitives: from Papyrus Brooklyn

Papyrus Brooklyn (originally *c.* 200 × 30 cm) probably came from the Theban tomb of a woman called Sonebtisy, which may have existed near that containing the 'Ramesseum Papyri' (see **3**). This is suggested by a list of some ninety-five servants of Sonebtisy which was made on the back of this administrative roll in the 13th Dynasty (*c.* Sekhemreswadjtawi Sobekhotep (III)).

The text on the front was begun late in the reign of Amenemhat III, over a century earlier, and is a register of eighty fugitives, laid out on a set of ruled guidelines. This register is a

---

[4] Literally 'the one serving (on a quarrying expedition)'.

[5] Literally 'The protector from the scorpion goddess': a warder-off of scorpions.

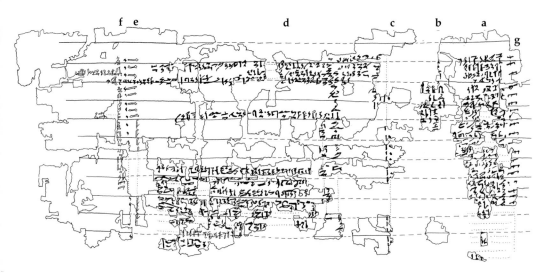

Papyrus Brooklyn (H. 30 cm).

summary of three reviews of cases in years 10, [20(?)] and 31, all of which concern people who fled the labour duty imposed by the governmental 'Office of (enforced) Labour'. The individual case entries are in columns which contain: (a) the fugitive's name, (b) his place of origin or the place or person from which he had escaped, (c) a determinative marking gender, and (d) the details of relevant administrative orders from the 'Great Enclosure', the central labour base. A fugitive would be condemned to permanent labour, or, if he escaped, his dependants would serve instead until he was caught (as happens in **33c**). The second case given here is one of the most detailed: in it we learn that one Dedusobek fled on the day of being called for duty with the help of a skipper, who is cursed for his complicity.

Much later the cases were again reviewed and three further columns added: in (e) was recorded whether the fugitive had been captured ('here'), had returned voluntarily ('returning'), or was still at large ('being/to be brought'). Beside these entries are a set of check marks. Then a statement was made of the cases' official closure by various scribes of the vizier (f), and an abbreviation of the word 'closed' was placed before column (a) as a summary of this: (g).[1] For Dedusobek no such statements could be made. Around this time two decrees were also copied on to the roll, being inserted upside down in the remaining blank spaces. One was placed before column (a), and the other, which is **26**, underneath (d).

33a

      (g) Closed

      (a) Sabs' son Montuhotep

      (b) The orchard-[land of .....]

      (c) [man]

      (d) (an order) was issued to the Great Enclosure, year 31,[2]

---

[1] It is also possible that these columns refer to the documents about the cases rather than the fugitives themselves. This interpretation may be preferable.

[2] The preceding phrase was written out only once at the top of the page; in subsequent lines only varying elements were written.

month 3 of Shemu, day 5, for (his) being given to the farmlands together with his dependants for all time [in accordance] with the ruling of the court.

(e) HERE /

(f) STATEMENT BY THE SCRIBE OF THE VIZIER, DEDUAMEN: IT IS CLOSED.

33b

(g) –

(a) Khusobek's son Dedusobek

(b) The dependants [of .....]

(c) [man]

(d) (ditto), day 9, to say (that he has been) handed over to the 'Office of Labour' [on this day], and carried off for joining on his day (for labour duty) with the accursed Skipper of the Treasury, the accursed Deduamen's son Montuhotep.

(e) TO BE BROUGHT /

(f) –

33c

(g) Closed

(a) Sainhur's [daught]er Teti

(b) The scribe of the farmland of Thi[nis]

(c) woman

(d) (ditto), to release (her people) in the law-court, being (an order) issued in order to execute against her the law pertaining to one who flees without doing his labour-duty.

(e) HERE /

(f) STATEMENT BY THE SCRIBE OF THE VIZIER, DEDUAMUN: IT IS CLOSED.

33d

(g) Closed

(a) Wabet's son Resnakht

(b) The scribe of the farmland of Khen[y(?)]

(c) man

(d) (ditto), to execute against him the law of one who [wilfully] deserts [........]

(e) RETURNING

(f) STATEMENT BY THE SCRIBE OF THE VIZIER, AMENYSONEB: IT IS CLOSED.

34 Letters home: from the Heqanakht Papers

The Heqanakht papers are one of the most remarkable finds from the Middle Kingdom, made during excavations in the intact tomb of Meseh in the cliffs overlooking Deir el-Bahri at Thebes. Meseh was one of four people who had small burials in the courtyard of the tomb of Ipi, a vizier of Nebhetepre Montuhotep (II), and this position suggests that he was roughly contemporary with that king. Amongst the debris thrown into the tomb-shaft before it was sealed was a mass of crumpled papyri, which included a collection of letters and accounts connected with a man called Heqanakht.

Heqanakht was apparently the priest for the funerary cult of Ipi, and the letters were written to his household at Thebes while he was on business in the north. It has been suggested that his deputy Merisu, while acting for him at Ipi's tomb, took the letters and other documents with him and stored them there; soon afterwards, at the funeral of Meseh, they were discarded. All show signs of having been read, except one letter (not included here) which was still sealed; it was addressed to a neighbour, but presumably had been sent via Merisu who neglected to forward it. Another of the documents mentions years 5 and 8 of an unnamed king: Ipi must of course have been dead by this date, so the years probably belong to the reign of Nebhetepre's successor, Sankhkare Montuhotep (III). The two letters included here were written in the course of a single summer, perhaps that of l949 BC, **34a** just after Heqanakht left home in August, and **34b** a little later, early in September. The handwriting may be that of a professional letter-writer, but could well be Heqanakht's own.

Heqanakht's 'signature' (H. 4 cm).

The letters produce a remarkable sense of their sender's individuality: an elderly man, rather impatient, fussy, with a keen business sense, and capable of changing his mind in mid-sentence. The vividness of his family's squabbles has formed the basis for an Agatha Christie novel, *Death Comes as the End*, whose title is taken from a line of the 'Teaching of Ptahhotep' (**15**, maxim 18). The other *dramatis personae* are as follows:

The household

The five sons of Heqanakht, in order of age:

Merisu, his eldest and deputy, in charge of the household;
Sahathor, who accompanied his father and acts as courier between him and the family;
Sanebniut;
Inpu, rather younger than his brothers, and picked on by Merisu;
Snefru, the youngest, and a spoilt favourite.

Ipi, Heqanakht's mother;
Hotepet, a female relative, perhaps a sister or aunt, who is not liked by Merisu;
Nefret, perhaps a favourite daughter;
Iutenheb, Heqanakht's second wife and a source of conflict;
Senen, a family maid;
various other daughters and maids;
Heti's son Nakht, a family servant and a subordinate of Heqanakht's.

Friends and neighbours

Hau the younger, a land-owning neighbour, from whom Heqanakht rents land;
Hrunefer, a neighbour and an official superior to Heqanakht;
Khentikheti, the son of Ipi the younger, perhaps a fellow funerary priest, who has accompanied Heqanakht to the north, and from whom he rents land.

Locations

Nebsyt, the village in which the household lives, probably on the Theban plain close to Deir el-Bahri;

Khepshyt, a region of well-watered land on the floodplain;

Per-Haa, an estate ('The Estate of Haa') in Khepshyt on the floodplain, where Heqanakht farmed land;

[...]wi, a place with a farm of Heqanakht's.

In **34a**, Heqanakht instructs Merisu about preparations for the coming agricultural year. These include paying the rent, which has just been negotiated, for 30(?) arouras of land in Per-Haa, and renting additional land, if Merisu considers it advisable. Warnings follow to Merisu against appropriating any of the grain reserved to pay rent on another area of land, together with a complaint that the grain sent to Heqanakht was old. The only land actually owned by the funerary priest seems to have been a lot in [...]wi, of unknown size. The rest of the letter is concerned with domestic matters, in particular the family's antagonism towards his new wife.

34b begin on a more personal note, to reassure his mother, but quickly turns to rebuke the family which has obviously been troubled by its low rations. Heqanakht tells them that, with the low inundation, they are greedy to expect anything else; where he is in the north things are far worse (according to him). From the papyrus we can see that as he set their spartan rations, he realised that he was being overgenerous to his young favourites among the family and altered the figures quite drastically. Next, Merisu is given instructions about the farming, which conerns 20 arouras rented from Khentikheti's property. His previous suggestion (made in **34a**) that extra land be rented from Hau the Younger in Khepshyt has clearly been followed, and he sends some copper to help pay its rent. The end of the letter is particularly brusque, as he complains again about the abuse his new wife has suffered at the hands of the family, who regard her as a slut. He writes for her to be sent to him in the north.

34a

(Address:)   Sent by the funerary priest Heqanakht to his household of Nebsyt.

A message from the funerary priest Heqanakht to Merisu: 'As for all that can be inundated in our land: you're the one who is farming it – pay attention, all my people, and (especially) you! Look, I reckon you responsible for it – be very strenuous in farming! Take great care! Watch over my seed-corn! Look after all my property! Look, I reckon you responsible for it. Take great care with all my property!

Make sure that Heti's son Nakht is sent down, with Sanebniut, to Per-Haa, to farm 30(?) arouras of land for [us] on rent; they shall take the rent for it from the *Men*-cloth woven there. Now, if they've (already) sold the emmer which was in Per-Haa, they shall pay (the rent) with this as well; so you'll have no more to do with the *Men*-cloth, about which I said, "Weave it; they shall take it to be sold in Nebsyt, and they'll rent land for its price."

Now, if you'd like to farm 20 arouras of land there, farm it! You'll find land – 10 arouras of land for emmer and 10 arouras for northern barley – from the [good] land of [Kh]epshyt. Don't go down on to (just) anyone's land! You shall request it from

Hau the Younger. If you don't find any with him, then you shall go before Hrunefer; he'll put you on well-watered land of Khepshyt.

Now, look, when I'd come south to here (where you are),[1] you counted out for me the rent of 13 arouras of land in northern barley a[lone]. Take great care! Watch out you don't purloin a (single) sack of northern barley from it, like someone sowing with his own northern barley, because you've (already) made renting them with the northern barley and seed awkward enough for me.

Now, look, as for him who sows with the northern barley – as for the 65 sacks of northern barley from 13 arouras of land, that is (only) 9 sacks from each aroura of land – look, that's not a "bad squeeze"![2] Look, 20 arouras of land add up to 100 sacks of northern barley. Take great care! Watch out you don't get ambitious about (even) one sack of northern barley from it! Look, this isn't the year for a man to get rebellious with his master, or his father, or his brother.

Now, as for all that Heti's son Nakht will have done in Per-Haa – look, I've reckoned rations for him for one month only: one sack of northern barley. I shall reckon another second one, of 5 gallons of northern barley, for his dependants on the first day of the month. Look, if you overstep this, look, I'll treat it as purloining by you. Now, as for what I've (just) told you – "Give him a sack of northern barley for the month" – you'll give him only 8 gallons for the month (instead). Take great care!

Now, what's the idea of having Sahathor come to me with old dried up northern barley, from Djedisut,[3] without giving me the 10 sacks of northern barley in new good northern barley? So, you're happy, eating good northern barley, while I'm neglected,[4] aren't you? Now, the boat's come home for you, while you're acting so badly! If you'd have had the old northern barley brought to me, in order to keep the new northern barley together, what could I have said? (Nothing but:) "How good that is!" But if you won't allot me one (gallon) of (good) northern barley, I'll not allot you one – for eternity!

Now, I've been told: "Snefru is [lazy(?)]"! Take great care of him! Give him provisions! Also greet Snefru, as Khentikheti says,[5] a thousand times, a million times! Take great care! Write

---

[1] This refers to an incident after a previous business trip.

[2] i.e., to expect this much rent isn't asking too much.

[3] A name for Memphis.

[4] A stroke was placed beside this word, perhaps to add emphasis.

[5] i.e., Khentikheti also sends his greetings.

to me! Now, as for my inundated land, he shall farm (it) with you and Inpu – in your care and Sahathor's. Take great care of him! You shall send him to me after the farming. Have him bring me 3 sacks of wheat, together with what northern barley you can find – but (only) what is in excess of the provisions for you until you get to harvest time. [Don't] neglect all that I've written to you. Look, this is a year for a man to help his master.

Now, as for all the affairs of my estate, and all the affairs of my plot in [...]wi – the one I sowed with flax (before) – don't let anyone go down on to it! Now, as for anyone who shall mention (using it) to you, you shall go on account of him and [farm it yourself (before he can)(?)]. Now, you shall sow this plot with northern bar[ley – don't] sow emmer there! Now, only if it turns out to be a high inundation shall you sow it with emmer.

Take great care of Inpu and of Snefru! You die by them and you live by them; take great care! Look, there's nothing more important than him in that house with you. Don't ignore this!

Now, make sure that the housemaid Senen is thrown out of my house – take great care – on whatever day Sahathor reaches you (with this letter). Look, if she spends one day (more) in my house – [watch it]! It is you who let her do evil against my new wife. Look, why must I nag you? What can she do against you, you five children?[6]

Also greet my mother Ipi, a thousand times, a million times! Also greet Hotepet and the whole household, and Nefret; now, what about this evil treatment of my new wife? You go too far. Are you appointed with me, as my arbitrator? You shall stop – how good that would be!

Also have an account brought of what is to be collected of the things from Per-Haa. Take great care! Don't be neglectful!'

34b

(Address:)   Sent by the funerary priest Heqanakht
               to his household in Nebsyt.[7]

A son speaks to his mother, the funerary priest Heqanakht to his mother Ipi, and to Hotepet: 'How are you? Are you alive, prosperous, healthy? In the favour of Montu, lord of Thebes!' And to the whole household: 'How are you? How are you? Are you alive, prosperous, healthy? Don't worry about me. Look, I'm well and alive. Look, you are like the man who eats until

---

[6] He accuses his five sons of feeling threatened by Iutenheb, and of not protecting her from the malice of the maid, who presumably resented her as an intruder.

[7] Beside the address is a hieratic sign depicting a steering-oar, perhaps to indicate that the letter was sent by boat.

sated, having hungered until his eyes sank in. Look, the whole land is dead, (yet) [you] have not hungered. [Lo]ok, I came here southwards (to where you are), and I fixed rations for you, well. [Now], the inundation is not [very high], is it? Look, our rations are fixed for us in measure with the inundation. Endure (this), each one (of you)! Look, I've managed to keep you alive up to today.

List of rations for the household:

Ipi	8 gallons	(Insert:) For
her servant		Sanebniut rations
Hotepet		shall be measured
her servant	8	from his northern
Heti's son Nakht	8	barley – it is on his
and his dependants		threshing floor –
Merisu, his dependants	8	until he departs to
Sahathor	8	Per-Haa.
Sanebniut	7	
Inpu	5,4[8]	
Snefru	8,4	
Sainut	4	
Mi's daughter Hotepet	9,5	
Nefret	4.5,3.5	
Satweret	2	

Total: 7 sacks, 9.5 gallons

If[9] – watch out that you're not angry about this! Look, the whole household is like my children; everything is mine.'

A message: 'Being half alive is better than death altogether. Look, one should say "hunger" (only) about (real) hunger. Look, they are starting to eat people here. Look, they haven't been given such rations in any place (here). Until I reach you, you shall bear yourself with strong hearts! Look, I shall spend the Shemu[10] here.'

Message by the funerary priest Heqanakht to Merisu, and Heti's son Nakht, the subordinate: 'You shall give these rations to my people, while they are working. Take great care! Hoe all my land, sift with a sieve and hack up with your noses in the work! Look, if they are vigorous, you shall be thanked, and I shall not give you a nagging. Now, the rations, about which I've written to you, shall be begun to be given out on the first of Khentikhetiperti[11] for the first of the new month. Don't neglect

[8] Before the letter was sent, Heqanakht altered the rations, reducing those allotted to the young; he forgot to alter the total. A note was inserted that the household grain should be issued to Sanebniut only after he had gone to work. Iutenheb is presumably omitted from the list as Heqanakht intends her to come to him in the north.

[9] Heqanakht changes his mind and starts a fresh sentence.

[10] i.e., another three months.

[11] The name of the second month of Shemu.

the 20 arouras of land which are in the neighbourhood, given to Ipi the Younger's son Khentikheti for his hoeing (them). Be very vigorous! Look, you're eating my rations.

Now, as for all the property of Inpu which is in your possession – give it (back) to him. As for what's destroyed – repay it to him! Don't make me write to you about this another time. Look, I've written twice.

Now, if Snefru wants – is (still) wanting to be in charge of those bulls, you should put him in charge of them. Now, he didn't want to be with you, farming, and coming and going. And he didn't want to come with me. Whatever he does want, you shall make him content with what he wants.

Now, as for anyone, of either the men or the women, who shall reject these rations, let him come to me, here with me, and live as I live! – now, no one comes to me here, (do they?).

I told you: "Don't keep a friend of Hotepet away from her, neither her hairdresser, nor her assistant(?)." Take great care of her! O may you prosper in everything accordingly! Yet, you have not loved her (in the past). You shall now cause Iutenheb to be brought to me. I swear by this man – I speak of Ip(i) – anyone who commits a misdeed against the sex of my new wife, he is against me and I against him. Look, this is my new wife; what should be done for a man's new wife is (well) known. Look, as for anyone who acts to her like I have acted – would one of you be patient when his wife was denounced to him? I'll be (no more) patient (than you would)! In what way can I be at the same table with you? Shall you not respect my new wife?

Now, look, I've caused 24 debens of copper for land-rent to be brought to you by Sahathor. Now, let 20 arouras of land – in Per-Haa beside Hau the Younger – be farmed for us by (paying this) rent in copper, clothes, northern barley, [or] any[thing]; but it shall be after you've sold the oil and anything else there. Take great care! Be very vigorous! Be vigilant! Now, look, you are on good, well-watered land of Khepshyt.'

35 Trouble at home: a letter from a general

The provenance of this letter is unknown, but may have been Thebes; the hand suggests a date in the late 11th Dynasty. It is written on both sides of a sheet of papyrus, 26 x 18 cm, which was then folded into a packet 8 x 4 cm. In it a general questions Kay, apparently his father-in-law, following a complaint from his wife that supplies sent by him via Kay and his children have not reached the household. The general suspects that Kay's second wife is responsible, having turned against her stepdaughter.

(Address:) […] Kay.

A message from the General Nehesu to the […] of […], Kay: 'How are you, how are you? Are you alive, prosperous and

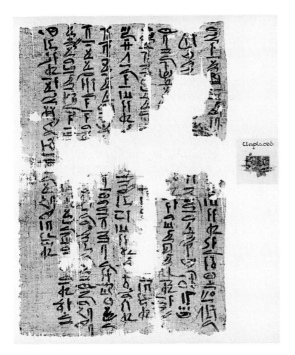

The general's letter (26 × 18 cm).

healthy? Your state is [like the living, a million] tim[es]! May Montu, Lord of Thebes assist you, and all the gods – may they make for you a million years of life, prosperity and health, and [....], as I desire. What about that message for me from Senet, saying, "No food is brought to me"? Lo[ok, I sent ... sacks of grain] to my household, and ten sacks to you. Have Kay's daughter [..]usenet and Kay's son Nefersesh brought them from the cargo-ship? [If they have not] you shall bring them (yourselves). Another thing: look, (it's) a delivery in full: so what about [letting] yourself be turned against your daughter? What you've done will be to kill her, by [...]'s not giving that grain to [my] household! Now, look, I know the character of a stepmother: are you following your wife's wishes in killing my household?

Can I be confident that I've given my household provisions when I'm sent to, about there being no provisions? Cause the cargo-ship to return, once it has reached me.'

36 A family will: the transfer deed of Wah

This document (57 x 32 cm) was drawn up in the second year of one of Amenemhat III's successors, perhaps Amenemhat IV. It was presumably placed in an archive at el-Lahun,

108

The transfer deed of Wah (57 × 32 cm; adapted from Möller, *Hier. Lesestücke* I, 17).

and when found it was still folded and sealed. In it the priest Wah makes provisions for his wife to inherit his property, perhaps on the occasion of his marriage. At a later date an extra line was added which shows that a son had been born by then. It may also imply, from his appointment of a guardian, that Wah did not expect to live long enough to raise his son himself.

The will is prefaced by a copy of the document, dated some six years earlier, which bears witness to Wah's legal ownership of property formerly owned by his brother, Ankhreni. Ankhreni was an official of some wealth, able to afford a funerary chapel at el-Lahun (or Abydos), which is known from one surviving offering table. By chance we also have a deed of sale from year 29 of Amenemhat III, in which Ankhreni received the services of several Asiatic servants: these are presumably the same as those bequeathed by Wah to his wife. It is hard to escape the impression that Wah's prosperity depended on his brother's generosity. The 'house of Wah' is mentioned in a letter from el-Lahun (**29b**) as a matter requiring attention: it might be that this transfer of property did not go smoothly.

(Label written on verso, after the document was folded:)
The transfer deed made by the priest in charge of the phyle, Wah.

COPY OF THE TRANSFER DEED MADE BY THE TRUSTED SEAL-BEARER OF THE DIRECTOR OF WORKS, ANKHRENI.
Year 44, MONTH 2 OF SHEMU, DAY 13:
Transfer deed made by the Trusted Seal-bearer of the Director of Works, Shepset's son Ihisoneb, named Ankhreni, of the northern district:

All my possessions in country and town to my brother, the priest in charge of the phyle of Sopdu, Lord of the East, Shepset's son Ihisoneb, named Wah. All my household to this brother of mine. This was placed as a copy in the office of the second Reporter of the South in year 44, month 2 of Shemu, day 13.

Year 2, MONTH 2 OF AKHET, DAY 18:
Transfer deed made by the priest in charge of the phyle of Sopdu, Lord of the East, Wah: I am making a transfer deed for my wife, a woman of the Left Side, Sopdu's daughter Sheftu, named Teti – of everything that my brother, the Trusted Sealbearer of the Director of Works, Ankhreni, gave to me, with all the goods as they should be – of all that he gave me. She herself shall give (it) to any of her children that she shall bear me, that she wishes.

I am giving her the 3 Asiatics which my brother, the Trusted Seal-bearer of the Director of Works, Ankhreni, gave to me. She herself shall give them to any of her children that she wishes.

As for my tomb, I shall be buried in it, and my wife also, without letting anyone interfere with it.

Now, as for the rooms that my brother, the Trusted Seal-bearer Ankhreni, built for me, my wife shall live there, without letting her be cast out of it by any person.

It is the deputy Gebu who shall act as guardian to my son.[1]

Namelist of the people in whose presence this was done:
The Scribe of the Pillars, Kemnu.
The Temple Door-keeper, Ankhtifi's son Ipu.
The Temple Door-keeper, Soneb's son Soneb.

37 A troubled inheritance: a son's statement of claim

This sheet of papyrus (30 x 22 cm) also comes from an official archive at el-Lahun. It is probably complete apart from the fragmentary top line, which mentions 'Peace-of-Senwosret-true-of-voice' and someone from the 'Left Side', called 'Sonebebu'. This was perhaps the heading of the following statement in which a son lays claim to a sum promised to his father in exchange for an official position; selling offices and the endowments which provided their salaries was a fairly common practice. The statement was presumably one of a group of papers kept as relevant to the ensuing court case. It illustrates two features of the legal system: its reliance on word of mouth (backed up by officially sanctioned transcriptions and witnesses) and its concern for 'contenting' contestants, rather than obtaining a conviction.

[The .....] of the Left Side, Sonebebu['s son(?) ... of] Peace-of-Senwosret-[true-of-voice ... ...] office (?). This is what his son says: 'My father made a transfer deed concerning the office of priest in charge of the phyle of Sopdu, Lord of the East, which

---

[1] This sentence was added later by another scribe.

was his, for the scribe in charge of the seal, of the Left Side, Iyemiatibi. He said to my father: "I am giving you the principal and bearing all the obligations, which are yours," so he said. Then my father was questioned by the Overseer of Fields Mersu, as deputy for the member of the officiate, saying: "Are you content with the giving of the aforementioned principal to you, an[d the bearing] of all the obligations, which have been assessed for you, [in] payment for your office of priest in charge of the [phyle]?" Then my father said: "I am content." The statement of the member of the officiate: "The two men shall be caused to take an oath, saying "[We] are content." [Then] the two men were called to swear by the lord l.p.h.[1] in the presence of the Count [...., by] the Overseer of Fields Mersu, as deputy for the member of the officiate.
Name list of the witnesses in whose presence this was made:
The scribe Iyem[iatibi(?)]
Ditto Py[...]
Ditto [...]au

Now, my [father arrived at the point of de[ath, and the obstacles concerning the principal had not been removed for him. M[y] father said to me when he was il[l: "If] you aren't given the principal that the scribe and Seal-bear[er Iy]emiatibi swore to me, you [sha]ll petition the official, who shall adjudicate, about it. So the principal shall be given to you" – so he said. I have made petition to him who acts [as...] here abou[t giving me] that which fell to the scribe in charge of the seal Iyemiatibi, [immediately (?)].'

38   A house census from el-Lahun

These papyri (32 x 15 cm, 23 x 13 cm and 32 x 32 cm) were found rolled up together and still sealed at el-Lahun (see **28**). They document the fluctuating size of a soldier's household into the 13th Dynasty, although they were not part of a population census but were drawn up to record the nature of the household for legal purposes (such as property transfer and inheritance: **38c** is a copy made as part of a document written in year 5 of Amenemhat V). The variation from three to eight members is probably fairly representative, as is the size of the family, who would have occupied a house some 15 x 20 m. **38a** records Hori's newly established family, which increased after the death of his father (**38b**); shortly after Hori's death, in **38c**, the household was headed by his still-unmarried son.

38a

[...(date(?))...]
[Made in the off]ice of the vizier, in the census-tent, [in the presence] of the Chief of the Tens of the South, Sery,
by the Steward and Accountant of Cattle, Nebpu, his servant [....],

---

[1] i.e., an oath in the king's name, in the presence of the mayor of el-Lahun.

the scribe of the judge Soneb [(from)(?)...],
and the domestic servant Senbebu:
The household-list of the soldier Djehuti's son Hori [of the
second (band)] of troops rais[ed up (for service), of the ...ern
Sector]:
his wife, Satsopdu's daughter Shepset – a woman of the Left
Side
her son Snefru – newborn[1]

38b

The household-list of the soldier Djehuti's son Hori, [of] the
second (band) of troops raised up (for service), of the [...ern
Sector]:
his wife, Satsopdu's daughter Shepset – a woman of the Left
Side
his son, Snefru[2]

his mother, Harekhni	her daughter, Isis
her daughter Qatsennut	her daughter Rudet[2]
‹her daughter› Mekten	her daughter ‹Sat›snefru[2]

38c

Year 3, month 3 of Akhet day 25, under the Person of the Dual
King: Sekhemkare, may he live for all time and eternity!
Copy of the household-list of the soldier, Djehuti's son Hori's
son Snefru, whose father was of the second (band) of troops
[raised up (for service) of the ...ern Sector]: his mother,
Satsopdu's daughter Shepset – a priestess of the Left Side
his father's mother Harekhni

his father's sister Qatsennut	Freewomen of the town of the
his father's sister Isis	necropolis-workers of the
his father's sister Satsnefru	Northern Sector

They are entered under the household-list of his father in year 2.[3]

39 Dogs

39a

Dogs are shown in the company of kings, officials and labourers, both as workers and pets.
The dogs of King Wahankh Intef (II) are shown at his feet on a stela (95 x 145 cm) in his
Theban funerary chapel. Their names are Berber, and are written beside them, three with
translations into Egyptian:

---

[1] As in inventories the determinatives are arranged in a separate sub-column (e.g., **33**(c), **37**). Here the
determinative is replaced by the word 'newborn'.

[2] The determinatives show that the individual was still a minor.

[3] This seems to refer to a list, now lost, from the previous year when Hori was still alive, and when these
relatives had already joined the household.

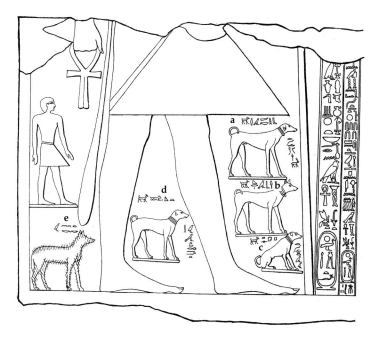

The 'Dog stela' (H. 95 cm; from Möller, *Hier. Lesestücke* III [17a]).

(a) Behkai (*Bhk3j*), that is to say: Gazelle.

(b) Abaqer (*3b3qr* which has been recognised as an Old Berber word meaning 'hound').

(c) Pehtes (*Phts*), that is to say: Black One.

(d) Teqru (*Tqrw*), (that is to say): *Khenfet*-kettle.

(e) Tekenru (*Tknrw*).

From other monuments come the names of various officials' dogs, often shown sitting under their masters' chairs:

39b

From an 11th-Dynasty funerary stela from Koptos:

Hemu-(em)-ma (*Ḥmw-(m)-m3*), 'The-tail-(literally steering-oar)-is-as-a-lion's'.

39c

One of five dogs belonging to a hunter, who pursued fugitives from the State in the Western Oases. The animal is depicted on his funerary stela found 17 km north of Luxor:

Diunu (*Djw-nw*), 'The-fifth'.

39d

From a stela of an Overseer of Quarry-works in his late 11th-Dynasty tomb at Thebes:

Ne-mereni (*N-mr.n=j*), 'I-don't-like'.

39e

The dog of the nomarch Djehutihotep, from his tomb at el-Bersha (see **24**).

Ankhu ('*nḫw*), 'Living-(i.e., lively?)-one'.

The dog of Count Djehutihotep, walking underneath his owner's carrying-chair. From a fragment of the nomarch's tomb at el-Bersha, now in the British Museum (BM 1147; H. 33 cm).

39f

The dog of Count Sonebi (see **21**):

Tjau-ne-ankh-ne-Sonebi (*T3w-n-'nḫ-n-Snbj*), 'Breath-of-life-for-Sonebi'.

39g

A dog shown on a very early 12th-Dynasty coffin from Asyut, being led on a leash by the deceased, Khu:

Meniu-pu (*Mnjw-pw*), 'He's-a-shepherd'.

39h

From Thebes come fragments of a small coffin for a bitch (25 × 70 cm). It is exactly like a plain square human coffin with bands of inscriptions giving the deceased's name. The two surviving bands read:

The Blessed one before the great god Aya (i.e., 'Woofer'?).

An offering-which-the-king-gives to Osiris, lord of Busiris:
an invocation offering of bread, beer,
flesh and fowl for the blessed one,
beloved of her mistress, Aya.

40 A monument for a favourite harpist

On the stela of the Overseer of Priests Iki, from his cenotaph at Abydos (late 12th to 13th Dynasty), a fat harpist is shown performing a funerary song in praise of the tomb:

O this tomb! you were built for festivity,
you were planned for happiness!

The harpist, Neferhotep, was given his own monument on a much smaller stela (53 × 26 cm), which was placed in the cenotaph, doubtlessly with Iki's permission. It was commissioned by one of his friends, Nebsumenu, a carrier of bricks, and carved by a draughtsman who left his signature at the bottom (c). The same man seems to have carved Iki's stela, and he presumably gave his services for the humble Neferhotep as a friend. Without wealth and apparently without family, the harpist Neferhotep is one of the humblest people commemorated with such a memorial, which must have been a

a

b

c

The stela of the fat harpist Neferhotep (53 × 26 cm).

considerable expenditure for his friends. The characterful relief speaks for itself, and the phrase above it (b) expresses, to a rare degree, Nebsumenu's affection.

> (a)
> An offering-which-the-king-gives to Osiris, Lord of Abydos,
> and Horus son of Isis,
> that they may give an invocation offering of bread and beer,
> flesh and fowl,
> alabaster and linen,
> and everything good and pure
> for the spirit of the harpist
> Neferhotep, true of voice,
> born of the housewife Henu.
> It is his friend whom he loved,
> the Carrier of Bricks, Nebsumenu, who has made this for him.
> (b)
> Alas! give him love!
> (c)
> The draughtsman: Rensoneb's son Sonebau.

Religious life

Egyptian religion has been termed a 'metalanguage', used by the elite to comprehend the universe, since it embraces a great profusion of often contradictory images which do not form a single logically organised system. There is an absence of explicit written analysis which could be termed 'theology', and in the preserved evidence discourse about the gods is formulated primarily through hymns, rituals and representational iconography. The lists of book titles preserved in temple libraries of the Greco-Roman period sound more systematic, but it is uncertain whether any similar body existed by the Middle Kingdom, although some texts, such as the guides to the Netherworld (e.g., **52a**), display a degree of codification.

The hymns recited in temple ceremonies were recorded in various contexts, such as on monuments or as part of a lector-priest's library; some copies were kept for aesthetic rather than practical reasons, and they have considerable literary appeal. The example translated here (**41**) is a hymn to the god of the dead copied on to funerary stelae. It alludes to a body of mythical events, and narrative myths did exist, although their role in the written structuring of religious thought was limited. They must have been widespread orally, but in writing more encyclopaedic formulations of religious knowledge took precedence (such as the topographical list of attributes in **41**). The rare example given here (**42**) takes the form of a literary narrative, and as such shows a less monumental side of divinity than that presented by the grandiose eulogies of the hymns. However, despite the human-like frailties shown here, the contact between the gods and men was severely limited. The gods were the creators and upholders of the eternal cycle of the universe, which was governed by the order they instituted rather than by their direct intervention. Thus the temples were not places of personal worship but 'mansions' separated from the impurities of the world by enclosure walls. Temples were an integral part of the State administration. Individual contact with, and access to, the divine was a privilege of the king, derived from his partaking of divinity himself. While in ideology the king was the sole intermediary between the divine and the human, in the practicalities of religious ritual members of the elite obtained access through part-time priestly service; the priesthood was not a profession set apart from the rest of society. The other means of access to the divine was by the burial ceremonies which assimilated the dead with the eternal divine (these too may have been originally a royal prerogative). The religious life of the majority of the populace is an unknown factor. Their burials were rudimentary, although the presence of meagre grave-goods shows that an afterlife was envisaged. In this life their access to the temple gods was limited to witnessing festivals (cf. **48**). While a common man could summon the priest and request that an offering be made, he remained excluded from the activities; the temple cult was an embodiment of the ideal State order (as shown by **43**).

The essence of the State religion was the maintenance of the partnership of god and king in sustaining Maat and in destroying hostile forces (see **44, 46**). The royal nature of the cult was perhaps less strong in the case of minor or local gods such as Heqaib at Elephantine: he was an Old Kingdom count who was deified in the Middle Kingdom, and acquired a temple in the town. Funerary stelae and statues of local grandees were dedicated within the temple enclosure, some recording their endowments and their building works for the sanctuary; elsewhere such activities were attributed exclusively to royalty.

The cult was enacted with a tightly regulated calendar of daily, monthly and occasional feasts, and it is perhaps indicative of its nature that one of the few preserved festival rituals concerns the king (**45**). Nevertheless, side by side with this sense of divinity as an unalterable impersonal institution, there are traces of a belief in the gods as personal forces, which was perhaps more 'popular'. The two need not have been mutually exclusive: the literary texts which reflect the attitudes of the State cults include direct interventions by the gods in characters' lives, although these usually occur in distant places or distant times. It seems likely that the beliefs of the populace were centred less around the State pantheon than around local and domestic gods and ghosts (see illustration on p.129). There are few explicit references to this level of religion, but texts such as **47–8** reflect an individual's relationship with the divine, which allows intercession. (It may be significant that they come from a funerary context, where the human and the divine are closest.) Another major expression of piety was in the magical texts (**49**), which do not differ from those used in the State cult (**46**), but, unlike it, clearly envisage the numinous as having a direct influence on private individuals. Magic and religion were not differentiated as in the West. Dead relatives, whose cults were celebrated with rites, provided another means of access to quasi-divine power, and they also could be invoked for personal ends (**55–7**). The apparent preoccupation of Egyptian society with death is one aspect of its pervasive awareness of the numinous coexistent with the mundane, of the eternal coexistent with the transient living.

41 A hymn to Osiris

Funerary stelae contain many hymns, in particular to Osiris as ruler of the Netherworld. This hymn is attested on five Middle Kingdom stelae, as well as in eight later copies, in differing degrees of completeness and with several variants. A 12th-Dynasty stela in Cairo contains the fullest Middle Kingdom text, while two 13th-Dynasty ones now in the Louvre have thirty-four and thirty-three verses. The late 12th-Dynasty stela of Khentikhetiemhat in the British Museum has twenty-three verses, as does its duplicate in the Ashmolean, which was apparently made because the owner was dissatisfied with the craftsmanship of the first version. These show Khentikhetiemhat making an invocation; the hymn fills the rest of the stela.

The hymn is a eulogy, comprising an incantatory series of epithets, some of them symmetrically arranged according to the first word of each verse. This first stanza is an invocation and the second contains a catalogue of places expressing the extent of his lordship. The first half of the hymn ends with a stanza alluding to ceremonies which evoke the myth of the god's vindication by his son after his murder. A second invocatory stanza begins the second half and another topographical and ceremonial stanza acclaims him as ruler of both living and dead. The hymn concludes with a declaration of his vindication, made by his son.

Although it is found in a funerary context, the hymn was originally recited as part of the festivals at Abydos, rather than at burials, as is shown by the British Museum copy which has a slightly different version of the opening:

'Hail to you, O Osiris, Foremost of the Westerners
on this goodly day, on which you appear!'

A 19th-Dynasty stela provides eight further verses which, since they echo Old Kingdom funerary texts, may not be later accretions. In these the speech of Horus concludes with phrases also suggestive of a festal context:

'May you be well pleased with me on this day.
May you drive off my impediment; may you hear when I call you.
May you come forth due to all that I say to you, fair on this day.'

Worshipping Osiris: the spoken words of N;
he says:

'Hail to you, Osiris son of Nut;
lord of two horns, high of crown;
given the Great Crown;
joyful before the ennead;
for whom Atum fashioned reverence
in the hearts of men and gods,
the blessed spirits and the dead;

given rulership in On;
great of forms in Busiris;
lord of fear in the Two Mounds;
great of dread in Restau;
lord of reverence in Heracleopolis;
lord of power in Tenenet;
great of love upon earth;
lord of fair repute in the palace of the god;
great of appearances in Abydos;

given truth of voice before the entire ennead;
for whom slaughter was made
in the great Hall which is in Herwer;
whom the great powers dread;
for whom the great ones rise from their mats;
fear of whom Shu has caused;
reverence of whom Tefnut has created;
to whom the two Shrines of North and South come,
bowing down, so great is fear of him,
so strong is reverence of him.

This is Osiris! Sovereign of the gods;
great power of heaven;
ruler of the living;
king of those yonder;

whom thousands bless in Kheraha;
for whom the sunfolk rejoice in On;
lord of choice offerings in the Upper Houses;
for whom butchery is done in Memphis;
for whom the Night Offerings are done in Letopolis;
whom the gods see,
and give him praises;
whom the blessed dead see,
and make jubilation for him;
for whom multitudes have mourned in Abydos;
for whom those in the Netherworld rejoice.

Your son Horus has said: "I have come,
having smitten for you those who smote!"'

42 A fragment of myth: 'Horus and Seth'

Only two narrative myths are known from the Middle Kingdom, one preserved on a tattered papyrus, 40 × 15 cm, from el-Lahun (see **28**), the other an unpublished fragment (Papyrus Cairo CCG 58040). Such myths, though attested in texts, were perhaps a predominantly oral phenomenon; in the written formulation of religious knowledge they were not as central to the tradition as hymns and rituals. This has led some scholars to doubt the existence of narrative myths and to suggest that these surviving episodes were instead parts of magical spells. Since tales involving gods and mythical motifs are found at this period, there are few grounds for such doubt.

This example concerns two rival gods; Seth attempts to seduce Horus, the son of Osiris, but is about to be foiled by Horus' wise mother. The episode is preserved more fully in the New Kingdom satiric 'Tale of Horus and Seth', where the aim of Seth is to disgrace Horus in the contest for the kingship; by following Isis' advice, Horus avoids impregnation and Seth's semen is used to ensure that Seth is humiliated instead. Here, however, Seth appears to be motivated by desire, and utters one of the earliest recorded chat-up lines.

[..........]
And then the Person of Seth said
to the Person of Horus: 'How lovely your backside is!
Broad are [your] thighs(?) [and ....].'
And the Person of Horus said:
'Watch out; I shall tell this!'
[Then they returned] to their palaces.
And the Person of Horus said
to his mother Isis:
['Look,] Seth [sought] to have (carnal) knowledge of me.'
And she said to him 'Beware! Do not approach him about it!
When he mentions it to you another time, then you shall say to
    him:

"It is too painful for me entirely, as you are heavier than me.
My potency shall not match your potency," so you shall say to
   him.
Now, when he gives (his) potency to you,
you shall thrust your fingers between your buttocks.
Look, causing it to [....] for him is like [....].
Look, it will be sweet to his heart, more than [....].
[You shall then] catch the semen which has come from his
   member,
without letting the sun see it.'
[Then the Person of Seth said:
'Come, so I can see [you]
and [..........]'

43 The temple cult: from the 'Lament of Ipuur'

In the 'Lament of Ipuur' (see 12) a sage describes the chaos-stricken land and urges the 'Lord
to the Limit', whom he is admonishing, to recall the golden past. This is embodied by the
establishment of the State cults, which are described in terms of temple buildings, offerings
and priestly service (for which see also 28a).

'Remember the [building] of the shrine, the censing with
   incense,
the pouring water from the libation vessel at dawn.

Remember the fattened *Ra*-geese, the *Terep* and the *Set*-geese,
the laying of offerings to the gods.

Remember the chewing of natron, the preparing of white bread
by a man on the day of wetting the head.

Remember the setting-up of flagstaffs, the carving of offering
   stones,
while the priest is purifying the shrines
and the temple is plastered white as milk,
the sweetening of the Horizon,[1] the endowment(?) of offering
   loaves.

Remember the upholding of regulations, the correct ordering
   of dates,
the removing of him who enters the priestly service with
   impure body:
this is doing it wrongly;
this is destroying the heart [of him who does it(?)].

[Remember(?)] the day at the head of eternity,
your months (of service), the [....] and years, which are known.

---

[1] i.e., the sanctuary where the god dwells.

Remember the killing of oxen, the [.....],
[.....] of your best(?).

Remember the coming forth pu[re to a] man who has
   summoned you,[2]
the placing of a *Ra*-goose on the fire,
[.........].'

44 The daily ritual: a temple scene from the 'White Chapel'

Middle Kingdom temples were often of mudbrick with only elements of stone, unlike the
more elaborate and better-preserved New Kingdom examples which were built over them.
Reused blocks were found in an 18th-Dynasty pylon at Karnak and have been carefully

A scene from the side of one of the
outer pillars on the north of the White
Chapel (w. 64 cm).

[2] The man on priestly duty leaves the temple to answer a request for an offering to be
made on behalf of a non-priest.

The reconstructed White Chapel, from a drawing by H. Parkinson.

reassembled into the 'White Chapel'. This beautiful building was dedicated to the Theban god Amen by Senwosret I, and consists of a raised platform with a pillared processional shrine, called 'She who elevates Horus, the beloved of the Double Crown'. This name refers to its use in royal rituals, perhaps re-enactments of the coronation or jubilees (see **45**).

The chapel, like the temples, is decorated with scenes from the daily ritual in which the high priest offered to the god, whose awakening and feeding were accompanied by hymns similar in style to those of **7** and **41**. Each tableau presents a microcosm of the universal relationship between gods and mankind: at the top is the sky with stars, and a line at the base represents the earth. Between these boundaries mankind can be represented only by the king (see **4**), who is shown here kneeling before the ithyphallic Amen and offering wine. The accompanying texts are highly decorative and emblematic: the same phrases are constantly repeated on almost every surface.

This scene is from the side of one of the outer pillars on the north of the Chapel (W. 64 cm).

(Top:)
Nekhbet, the Shining of Nekhen,
lady of the South – may she give life and dominion!

(Over king:)
Horus: Living of Manifestations;
Dual king: Kheperkare;
Horus of Gold: Living of Manifestations,
beloved of Atum in the Great Mansion.

123

(Above king:)
Senwosret, given life for all time.

(Between figures:)
Giving wine.

(Over god:)
Word spoken by Amen-Re, lord of the thrones of the Two
  Lands:
'I have given all life, stability and dominion to my son
Kheperkare, before the ennead.'

(Beside god:)
Amen-Re – may he give all life, stability and dominion.

(Behind god:)
Protection, life, stability and dominion are with him, like Re.

(Base:)
Life, dominion, stability and the feet of this perfected god.

45 A royal ritual: from the 'Dramatic Papyrus'

Amongst the papyri from the 13th-Dynasty tomb of a lector-priest under the Ramesseum at Thebes (see 3) was a roll measuring 215 × 27 cm, whose beginning is lost. It contains a copy – presumably for professional use – of a ritual whose exact nature is uncertain. It is in honour of Senwosret I and is apparently to do with his assumption of the kingship either at coronation or jubilee (see also 44). At the bottom of the roll a series of vignettes with schematic figures shows the various episodes being performed. Each scene re-enacts a mythological incident, hence the modern title 'Dramatic Papyrus'. It is, however, only semi-dramatic, for the action is not organised in any narrative sequence but is a series of thematically related tableaux. The text is laid out in vertical columns of cursive hieroglyphs (from left to right). Each episode is described in one line, then come the speeches made by priests playing the various gods. In the lines below the dialogues the god so honoured is entered, then the items offered up and finally the place in which the act is imagined to be taking place.

 This scene is the thirty-third. It alludes to the revivifying embrace Horus gave to his dead father, Osiris which relates to the transference of the crown from the old king (Osiris) to the new (Horus). The ritual, like so much religious and literary thought, is structured by word-play.

It happens that a breast-plate (*qnj*) is brought forth by the lector priest.
This is Horus as he embraces (*qnj*) his father (Osiris), and turns before Geb.

A ritual in cursive hieroglyphs (H. 27 cm; from Sethe, *Dramatische Texte*, pl.20).

124

Horus › Geb Words spoken: 'I have embraced (*qnj*) my father who was weary, until	Horus › Geb he becomes well (*snb*)'
Osiris	Osiris
a breast-plate (*qnj*)	a *seneb*-plant
Pe	

The lector-priest: words spoken: 'Bring forth twelve breast-plates!'

46 A cursing ritual

This text is written in hieratic on a schematic alabaster figure of a bound captive (H. 15cm). It is one of five which were rumoured to have been found at Helwan and which have been dated to between Senwosret I and Amenemhat II. Similar objects are attested from Thebes and the frontier fortress of Mirgissa; they were used in State magic against enemies, being symbolically speared and cursed in rituals. On them was written an execration text which identified the figure with various hostile, or potentially hostile, groups. This example contains the last third of a text, beginning in mid-phrase. The full text, which was divided between three figures, begins with a list of various princes of Nubia, with derogatory descriptions. One of these seems to have been particularly infamous, since he is known also from other execration rituals:

'The ruler of Makia, (called) Wai,
born of his mother, of whom it is said "a (mere) calf" '.

Then come lists of Nubian countries and classes of Egyptians:

'all people, all patricians, all the folk,
all males, all eunuchs(?), all females,
all officials.'

This is followed by geographic areas and types of rebels. At this point the text starts on the figure shown here, which contains a list of Nubians, Libyans and two Egyptian rebels, one of whom is already dead and now a hostile spirit. His name makes it all but certain that he was the son of the vizier Intefiqer (see **26**). The last sign of the text, the determinative showing a bound captive which marks terms for enemies, is elaborately written as a final flourish.

The preceding figure's text concludes with the words:
and every rebel who plans to rebel
in this entire land:
all the Medjai of Webat-sepet;
all the Nubians of Wawat, Kush,
Shaat and Beqes,
[their] heroes, [their] runners,
all the Egyptians who are with them,
all the Nubians who are with them,

all the Asiatics who are with them,
all the families(?) of Upper and Lower Egypt(?), [who are with
   them]
the [...] who are with them,
all the [...] who are wi[th] them,
all the [for]eigners who are with [them];
all the Tjemhu of all the western hill-countries of the land of
   Tjemhu,
of He[..]kes and Hebeqes,
their heroes and their runners;
the dead man Intefiqer
born of Satsasobek,
and born of Intefiqer;
Senwosret, born of Imas.

An execration figure (H. 15 cm).

47 Two intercessory hymns: from the tomb of Intefiqer's mother

These two harpists' songs are from the Theban rock-cut tomb of Senet, the mother of the vizier Intefiqer under Senwosret I (see 22, 27). They are recorded on the south wall of the inner chamber beside scenes of the funeral and of sealing the tomb (H. 100 cm). The harpists are shown playing, with their titles above them in painted hieroglyphs, and above these are the songs themselves in vertical columns of cursive hieroglyphs, with the song-titles in a horizontal line. The text is riddled with holes and three columns of the first song and two of the second appear to have been painted out, like many parts of the tomb, including figures of Interfiqer (see 27). This damage and desecration makes the translation uncertain. On another wall of the chamber the same harpists, whom Interfiqer 'wanted every day', appear with songs invoking the vizier's revivification with mythological motifs:

'The inert one belongs to life!
The Vizier Intefiqer belongs to life!'

Here they make personal petitions to Hathor, the Lady of the West and goddess of rebirth, for his well-being. Although part of a vizier's funerary rituals, these songs give a glimpse of the relationship between ordinary men and the gods.

One whom his lord loves, one blessed
before the great god, lord of heaven,
the singer Dedumin,
begotten of Ihemi, true of voice.

Making of Jubilation
I make petition, so that you may hear, O Person of Gold!
I make supplication that your heart be turned to [me]!
Hail to you, Lady of Plague,
Sekhmet the great, Lady to the Limit!
Extolled one upon her father;
Eldest one before her maker;
foremost of place in the Bark of Millions,
free-striding in the cabin!
It is your a[rms(?)] which [give light],
your rays which illumine the two lands.
The two banks are under your counsel.
The sunfolk are your flock!

The harpists and their hymns for Intefiqer (H. 100 cm; from Davies-Gardiner,
Antefoqer, pl.29).

One blessed before Osiris, Lord of the West,
the singer Khuyet begotten of Meket.

Making of Jubilation

Hail to you, O Gold!
May you favour (me) since my occupation has been speaking to
  you!
I will be old and […] like a [miserable] one –
O powerful one, [of my knowing(?)]!
O Gold at your time of [listening(?)],
your hour of hearing!
You are green for my request to you!
May you release for me a vizier fair of speech!
You are the one who shall fashion the standard within your
  limbs; make fort[unate(?) …] with you!
It is [.....] which shall give a [good traversing (of eternity)(?)].

48 A washerman and his god: the stela of Hepet

A small stela (49 × 28 cm) from the northern cemetery at Abydos shows offerings being made to Ptah. This scene is accompanied by three lines of text above and three registers portraying the deceased's relatives below. It was a funerary monument (like **40, 53–4**), although the texts display no explicit funerary motifs. The stela shows an uncommon type of scene with a private person worshipping a god, which is exceptional before the 13th Dynasty. The man is of a relatively lowly rank: the wretchedness of a washerman's lot is vividly described in **17**. The family may have had some connection with Memphis, as the god is the memphite Ptah, and the washerman's only son has a name invoking the same god. The crude style of the stela, the poverty of its owner and the inclusion of the whole family are all characteristic of the 13th Dynasty.

The text:
The washerman Hepet
says: 'Hail to you Ptah, Lord of Life of the Two Lands.
I have come before you, that I may worship you.
I am a servant who does not forget his duty
in your festivals, truly!'

Between the figure of Ptah and the offering table:
For the spirit of Ptah, the ‹great› god, my lord,
that he may give me sweet breath for my nostrils!

The main scene includes a worshipper. The caption behind him shows that he is not Hepet himself, but Hepet's nephew:
Ankhuresu, begotten of Akhenimut.

Between Ankhuresu and the offering table is another figure offering bread, and kneeling:
His sister's husband Qutjat(?).

In the next register are shown:
His brother Neferhotep.

And facing him:
His mother, the housewife Ubenresh.
His sister, Aamet, true ‹of voice›.
His sister, Akhenimut(?), true ‹of voice›.
His friend, Pa[…].

Below them is:
His sister, Sonebesni.

And facing her:
His brother, Sahathor.
The housewife, Sonebesni.
His son, Sankhptah.
His sister, Itisoneb.

In the final register is a woman (his wife?):
Ibu.

And facing her:
His sister, Deduneshmet.
The housewife, Kemtu(?).
Nefer[…].

49 Magical spells to protect a child

Numerous magical spells are known, particularly from the 'Ramesseum library' (see **3**). No clear distinction can be drawn between them and religious practices; they are a form of practical theology, which is occasionally directly derived from temple rituals and funerary spells. Similarly, magical and medical texts exist side by side, intermingling (see **20**). The numinous coexists with other forms of knowledge.

These two spells are taken from a collection concerned with children which was copied on to a roll (217 × 16 cm) at the start of the New Kingdom; internal evidence, however, has assigned the spells themselves to the Middle Kingdom. The first is to be recited over an amuletic 'knot' to protect the child from a fever (**49a**). The spell concludes with an injunction to the poison to leave the body and is followed by instructions for the amulet and a note on the effectiveness of the spell. In the second (**49b**), which occurs several times in the papyrus with minor variations, the magician enacts a dialogue between the mother and the rising sungod designed to frighten off a ghost who is blamed for the illness. This may allude to a mythical precedent in which Re saved the infant Horus at the invocation of Isis.

A New Kingdom amulet, showing a hand and a crocodile (L. 3 cm).

49a

Spell for a knot
for a child, a fledgling:
Are you hot in the nest?

Are you burning in the bush?
Your mother is not with you?
There is no sister there ‹to› fan (you)?
There is no nurse to offer protection?
Let there be brought to me a pellet of gold,
40 bread pellets, a cornelian seal-stone,
(with) a crocodile and hand (on it),
to fell, to drive off this Demon of Desire, to warm the limbs,
to fell these male and female enemies from the West.
You shall break out! This is a protection.
ONE SHALL SAY THIS SPELL OVER THE PELLET OF GOLD,
THE 40 BREAD PELLETS, AND THE CORNELIAN SEAL-STONE,
(WITH) THE CROCODILE AND THE HAND.[1]
TO BE STRUNG ON A STRIP OF FINE LINEN;
MADE INTO AN AMULET;
PLACED ON THE NECK OF THE CHILD.
Good.

49b

A protective spell for guarding the limbs,
to be recited over a child when the sunlight rises:
You rise, Re, you rise!
Have you seen the dead who has come against her –
N (born) of N –
‹to› lay a spell on her,
using plans to seize her son from her embrace?
'May you save me, my lord, Re!'
so says N born of N.
'I shall not give you, I shall not give your charge
to a male or female robber from the West –
my hand upon you, my seal as your protection!'
so says Re as he rises.
May you break forth! This is a protection.

An ivory magical wand, part of a 12th-Dynasty magician's equipment. On it are
portrayed protective demons summoned by spells; note the crocodile (BM 18175;
L. 37 cm).

---

[1] Actual seal stones have been found, engraved with figures of a protective crocodile demon and a hand
representing the magician's gestures of power.

The other life

The modern image of the Egyptians as morbid is unfounded. Preparations for death may dominate the surviving records of their culture, but these sprang from a love for life, such as is revealed in a common phrase on funerary stelae: 'As you love life, as you shun death' (cf. **31c**). At a time when the average life expectancy was low (no higher than the twenties), death was an all-too-familiar enemy. The elaborate funerary rituals did not celebrate death, but sought to avoid destruction by the 'beatification' of the dead, by assimilating them with the divine (**51**). This was all-important: burial was a major expenditure, probably the major expenditure, of an official's life. The burial chamber would contain the coffin (see **1**), often with extensive texts (**1**, **52**), the mummy and mask, and grave goods including figures of servants, offerings and the like. The offering chamber for the cult was also highly decorated with representations of prosperity, such as **21–4**. The maintenance of a funerary cult required considerable endowments, and these preparations for immortality were entirely dependent on wealth. Nevertheless, 'a goodly burial' was a motif which wisdom literature presented in moral terms, as dependent on the dead man's virtues having created goodwill. The idea of death was an ethical force as well as a cause of great expenditure. The virtuous have never necessarily been the wealthy or successful, and there was a more abstract concept that immortality depended on virtue alone, regardless of social position (see **10**). Thus teachings proclaimed that a man might have escaped justice in this life, but judgement in the Netherworld was unavoidable, and that Truth was the only way of enduring (see **14–16**). The same dichotomy between worldly wealth and abstract value can be traced in descriptions of the Netherworld: many funerary spells presented the afterlife with familiar images of earthly prosperity (e.g., **52**), but others envisaged it as completely different from this world, with 'blessedness in place of water, air and sexual pleasure', and a place where everything is the reverse of life.

While all the tomb structures belong to the elite, the Middle Kingdom witnessed the extension of this privilege to a marginally greater section of society. This was a change both in economics and in belief which is seen most clearly in the 'cenotaph' chapels at Abydos. These commemorated the dead in the necropolis where Osiris was buried – the king of the dead, with whom all the dead were assimilated as 'the Osiris of N'. (This phenomenon parallels the less restricted access to the divine mentioned earlier.) The chapels were made of mudbrick and housed statues and stelae which proclaimed the dead man's virtue and achievements in order to evoke a pious response in the passer-by (e.g., **53–4**; also **40, 48**); occasionally, especially in the 13th Dynasty, these stelae belonged to relatively humble people (**40, 48**). Offerings were made as part of the funerary cult, but what the stelae required of the living was merely a spell – the spoken word which could summon up prosperity for the dead, and which has indeed endured longer than cult endowments. This relationship between the dead and the living (alluded to in **16**) was very vital: the beatified dead remained part of the community, keeping their individuality, and their potent ghosts could help the living. As a potential source of trouble (see **46, 49b**), or as an aid against distress, letters could be written to entreat their active goodwill in a time of crisis (**55–7**).

The Egyptian response to death was not simple: texts articulated death as paradoxically both a blessing and a bane (**50, 58**). The ultimate futility of funerary cults was as apparent then as now – the necropoleis were already full of open and abandoned tombs (cf. **59**) – but the importance of the tomb as a cultural statement lay in its role as the meeting place between the eternal and this world. In Egyptian thought the otherworld was the world of the ideal (cf. **50b**), not just a place where virtue could be vindicated, but the place where absolute Truth dwelled. For all its horror, death was regarded as the interface between the ideal and the actual world, which was an inevitable phenomenon in a cosmos riven by the separation of the divine and human spheres. In the declaration of the creator god in the Coffin Texts (**1**) man's awareness of mortality is a cause of his awareness of the gods, and even in the cynical Harpist's Song (**58**) it inspires the correct approach to life. The paradoxes of these texts reveal an intense perception repeated in the Michelangelesque epigram that although death destroys a man, the idea of death saves him.

50 The two aspects of death: from the 'Dialogue of a Man with his Soul'

From the 12th-Dynasty library which included the 'Tale of Sinuhe' and the 'Tale of the Eloquent Peasant' (the 'Berlin library': see **3**) comes the only manuscript of a complex literary text now known as the 'Dialogue between a Man Tired of Life and his Soul'. This dialogue explores the two aspects of death: its horror and its blessedness, as proclaimed in funerary texts and iconography. The first extract is from a speech of the soul who urges the man to consider the agony of death before he gives up life. The second comprises two lyrics from the man's final speech in which he extols death as a homecoming and the Netherworld as a place of perfect fulfilment. After these the soul announces that he is reconciled with the man, and a resolution is achieved between their opposing attitudes.

50a

'If you think of burial, it is agony;
it is the bringing of tears through making a man miserable;
it is taking a man from his house,
being cast upon the high ground.
You shall not come up again to see suns.
They who built in granite,
who constructed in fair pyramids, in fair works,
so that the builders should become gods –
their stelae have perished, like the inert ones',

those who have died on the shore for lack of a survivor,
the flood having taken its toll,
and the sun likewise,
to whom only the fish of the water's edge talk.
Listen to me! Look, it is good for men to listen.
Follow the happy day! Ignore care!'

50b

'Death is to me today
like a sick man's recovery,
like going outside after confinement.

Death is to me today
like the scent of myrrh,
like sitting under a sail on a windy day.

Death is to me today
like the scent of lotuses,
like sitting on the shore of Drunkenness.

Death is to me today
like a well-trodden path,
like a man's coming home from an expedition.

Death is to me today
like the opening of the sky,
like a man's grasping what he did not know.

Death is to me today
like a man's longing to see home,
having spent many years abroad.

Yet one yonder[1] is a living god,
punishing the wrongdoer's deed.

Yet one yonder stands in the (sun)bark,
distributing choice offerings thence to the temples.

Yet one yonder is a sage,
who cannot be prevented from appealing
to Re when he speaks.'

---

[1] i.e., the dead.

51 A goodly burial: from the 'Tale of Sinuhe'

In the 'Tale of Sinuhe' (see **3**) the protagonist despairs of returning to Egypt from his exile in Palestine. The new king, Senwosret I, summons him back with a letter which promises him an eternal homecoming: a goodly burial with full ceremonies and grave goods:

> Return to Egypt!
> For it is today that you have begun to be old, have lost your
>   manhood,
> and have thought of the day of burial,
> the traversing to blessedness.
>
> A night is assigned for you with oils,
> and wrappings from the hands of Tayet.
> A procession shall be made for you on the day of burial,
> with a mummy case of gold,
> a mask of lapis lazuli, a sky over you,
> and you on a hearse,
> with oxen dragging you,
> and chantresses before you.
> The dance of the Dead shall be performed at the mouth of your
>   tomb,
> and the funeral invocation recited for you;
> sacrifice shall be made at the mouth of your tomb-chamber,
> with your pillars, built of white stone,
> in the midst of the royal children's.

52 A map of Paradise: from Coffin Text Spells 466–7

The Coffin Texts contain spells describing a desirable afterlife, as well as those providing means of avoiding its dangers (see **1**). This was often a continuation of life in the Nile valley in the 'Field of the god Offering', which is portrayed in a map as a delta-like landscape, full of settlements, islands, canals and seas. The labels provide descriptions and the names of various features (the numerals in red ink are probably some unit of measurement). The map is found on several early Middle Kingdom coffins from el-Bersha with minor variations, and it survived essentially unchanged in the illustrated funerary papyri of the New Kingdom.

  This version is from the inner coffin of Gewa in the British Museum, which misses out several, often vital, words included in other copies (and marked ‹…› here). Only one of the accompanying spells, which describe life in this field, is copied on Gewa's coffin; the extract of Spell 467 translated here (**52b**) is taken from another coffin from el-Bersha.

52a The Map (Spell 466)

(a) BEING AS THE GOD OFFERING, LORD OF THE FIELD, WITH BREATH IN HIS NOSTRILS. HE CANNOT DIE.

(b) The town 'Beating'; **7**.

(c) Peaceful place; **8**.

(d) The Great (Town); **7**.

(e) This is a thousand leagues long and broad;
    it is called 'Horns of the Lady of Purification'.

(f) (The town of) the god Offering; **4**.

(g) Red place; **2**.

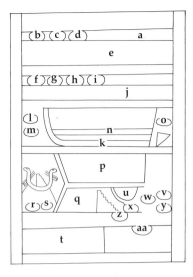

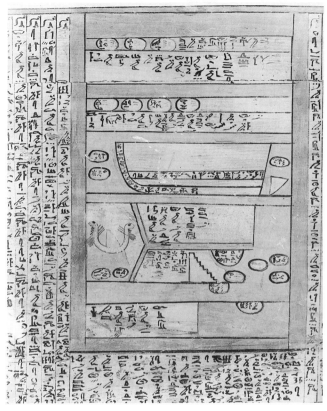

A map of Paradise, from the inner sides of the inner coffin of Gewa (BM 30840; H. 31 cm); from el-Bersha. He was a subordinate of the nomarch Djehutihotep.

(h) Inundated place; **3**.

(i) (The town of) the Lady of the Two Lands; **2**.

(j) 'The waterway of the White Hippopotamus';
it is a thousand leagues long, and its breadth has not been told.
There are not any fish or serpents in it.

(k) Its length is the length of heaven:
‹the waterway› of the god Offering, facing Upper and Lower Egypt.

(l) (The town) 'Mighty one'.

(m) (The town) 'United'.

(n) Ploughing and reaping the emmer and barley of the (estate) under the god.
There are no serpents at all in it.

(o) (The town of) the Mistress of the Winds.

(p) This is a thousand (leagues) long; and its width has not been told.
It is called 'Storm-raiser'.

(q) THOSE WHO ROW HIM (i.e., the god Offering): Imsety,
Hapy, Duamutef and Qebhsenuf.

(r) (The town of) provisions.

(s) (The town of the) Steps[1]

(t) This is the sea of the gods,
‹who put coolness in it for all the gods.›
Its length and its breadth are ‹not› told (even) to Osiris.

(u) The birthplace of the god, the town 'Beating'.

(v) (The town of) the Cow goddess; **3**.

(w) THE GREAT FIELD.

(x) 'The Basket'; **4**.

(y) (The town of) the Serpent Boat.[2]

(z) Lapis lazuli.

(aa) Women are here; ‹**4**›.

52b A description of life in the Field of Offering (from Spell 467)

I am the equipped one – Offering.
I am powerful with this very great magic
within this my body and this my place.
I am one who recalls to himself what he had forgotten.
I shall travel, plough and reap.
I am Offering in the city of the god.
I know the names of the towns, estates
and lakes within the Field of Offering in which I am.
I am mighty in it and I am glorious in it.
I shall eat in it and I shall travel in it.
I shall plough in it and I shall reap in it.
I shall make love in it and I shall be content in it.
I am glorious in it, even like Offering.
I shall sow seed in it and I shall travel in it.
I shall row in its lakes,
and I shall reach its towns,
even like Offering, at my (own) command.

53-4 Communication with the living: two funerary stelae

These stelae are among the most familiar Egyptian objects in museum collections. The majority come from necropoleis, although some may have been dedicated within temple enclosures (as at Elephantine). The major single group of Middle Kingdom examples comes from the necropolis of Abydos. There, in the 12th and 13th Dynasties, numerous chapels were built in the vicinity of the temple of Osiris, resembling a city of the dead. Some were parts of the actual burials of the local elite, while others were erected as mock tombs (hence the modern designation 'cenotaph') by officials visiting Abydos on a mission or on a pilgrimage. They range from humble solid structures to quite sizeable mudbrick vaulted chambers, either sealed (like a burial chamber) or left open to form a chapel with statues,

---

[1] The steps represent a terraced mound on which a god, often Osiris, dwells.

[2] The Serpent Boat is described as having 'a god in it' in later versions from New Kingdom 'Books of the Dead'.

offering stones and a courtyard. The common element is the stela placed in a niche on the outer wall; in the smallest it could be simply a flake of limestone, sometimes no larger than 12 cm. The aim of these structures was to associate the dead with the festivals of Osiris, so that they could partake of the temple offerings made to him, and on the stelae the deceased is often shown before a table of offerings. The texts give autobiographical accounts of the owner, varying from the very generalised (as in **13**) to the more specific (as here). They also include the formulae for funerary offerings desired by the deceased, with a prayer for passers-by to recite this. This appeal to all 'the living' was, of course, meant primarily for the literate: any communication by the dead elite was implicitly aimed at its own members still on earth. However, the stela of the steward Montuwoser, from the reign of Senwosret I, indicates that a wider, non-literate audience was also envisaged: its appeal includes the phrases: 'As for anyone who shall hear this stela .... As for any scribe who shall recite this stela....'

53 The stela of Sahathor

Sahathor's career began under Amenemhat II. His stela (H. 112 cm) contains a niche for a block statue, which has survived, as has an offering-table. The workmanship is fine, although the texts are not written very accurately. The main scene above the niche shows Sahathor with his wife (b) beside a pile of offerings. As well as the inscriptions translated here, there are two captions on the sides of the niche which describe how many expeditions he was sent on by the king, and how he supervised work on sixteen statues for the royal funerary complex.

(a)
An offering-which-the-king-gives to Osiris, lord of Busiris,
the great god, lord of Abydos:
an invocation offering of bread and beer,
flesh and fowl,
alabaster and linen,
incense and unguent,
at the Wag festival, at the festival of Thoth,
at the procession of Min(?), at the Burnt Offerings.
O you living who are upon earth,
who shall pass by this chapel ‹in› the necropolis,
going north, going south,
may you say, 'It is pure! A thousand of bread,
a thousand ‹of› beer,
a thousand ‹of› flesh and fowl,
oryx and gazelle,
and everything on which a god lives,
for the spirit of the blessed one,
the assistant treasurer Sahathor, true of voice.'

(b) (His wife)
The blessed one before Anubis who is upon his mount,
Meryisis, conceived of Hotepy.

(c)
I went on a mining expedition in my youth;
I suppressed the (local) chiefs, so that gold should be washed;

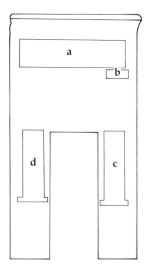

The stela of Sahathor
(H. 112 cm), with a cavetto
cornice, and a niche for a block
statue of the deceased.

I brought back turquoise; I reached the land of Nubia,
and the Nubians came bowing down,
for fear of the Lord of the Two Lands.
I went west,
and I travelled through its lands, and I brought back lily-
    plants(?).
As the lord lives, I speak truth!

One blessed before Anubis.

(d)
One whom his lord truly loves, a favourite of his;
who says what is perfect, repeats what is loved, and does what

the Lord of the Two Lands favours;
who repeats his conduct without neglect;
who is collected, free ⟨from⟩ forgetfulness;
who protects his boundary, beyond procedure;
who does his share, alert and free from laziness.

The assistant treasurer, Sahathor, true of voice,
one blessed before Wepwawet.

54 The stela of Nebipusenwosret

A fine limestone stela (H. 100 cm) shows the deceased with texts expressing his wish for
participation in the festivals of Osiris and Wepwawet (b), (c). The texts vary between a full
and an abbreviated form of Nebipusenwosret's name, which means 'Senwosret (III) is my
lord'. The autobiographical text (d) reveals that he was attached to the court at the capital
and never visited Abydos himself, but sent the stelae south with a priestly colleague
attending a ritual. His career spanned the reigns of Senwosret III and Amenemhat III.

(a)
Seeing the beauty of the perfected god
Khakaure, true of voice,
beloved of Osiris Wennefer, lord of Abydos,
beloved of Wepwawet, lord of the sacred land.

(b1)
Open be the sight of the Keeper of the Diadem,
the liegeman of the Great House, Nebipusenwosret,
that he may see Osiris, true of voice, before the two enneads,
as he rests in his palace,
his heart joyful for all time.
'I am content at this', says the desert.

(b2)
Open be the sight of the Keeper of the Diadem,
the liegeman of the Great House, Nebipusenwosret,
that he may see the beauty of Wepwawet in his beautiful
    procession,
as he comes in peace to his palace of sweetness of heart,
as the temple priesthood is in joy.

(c1)
Adoring Osiris at his beautiful festivals,
for all time and eternity.

(c2)
Adoring Wepwawet at his beautiful procession,
for all time and eternity.

(d)
Words spoken by the Keeper of the Diadem,
the liegeman of the Great House, Nebipusenwosret,
who grew as a child
at the feet of the king,
a pupil of Horus, lord of the palace:

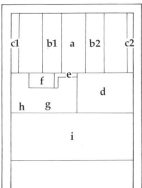

The stela of Nebipusenwosret (H. 100 cm).

140

'I acted as the Friend bearing the King's foot-ewer at the Feast
  of Years,
under the Person of Horus: Mighty of Power.
I acted as Great One of the Tens of the South and priest of the
  royal toilet at the Jubilee
under the Person of the Dual King: Nimaatre, may he live for all
  time!
This stela came south with the lector-priest Ibi,
when the temple priesthood came to see the king
at his festival, beautiful for all time.'

(e)
‹An offering-that-the-king-gives to› Osiris and Wepwawet,
and the gods of Abydos, that he (sic) may give every good thing
to the spirit of the Keeper of the Diadem,
Nebipu, true of voice.

(f)
An invocation-offering of Osiris' giving
to the spirit of the blessed one, Nebipusenwosret.

(g) (labels on the offerings)
Food-offerings:
A thousand of bread.
A thousand of beer.
A young long-horned ox.
A young *gu*-ox.

(h)
His beloved brother Pepy true ‹of voice›.

(i)
The Keeper of the Diadem, the liegeman of the Great House,
  Nebipusenwosret,
says to the temple priesthood of Abydos
and of his (i.e., Osiris') chapels of the Dual King:
'The king shall flourish in your life,
the monuments of your local god shall endure for you,
you shall be in the favour of your sovereign,
you shall hand over your offices to your children,
your offspring shall be enduring in your seats,
your offices of all time,
you shall not hunger, you shall not thirst –
the great god has ordained that you exist on earth in his favour –
and you shall not be imprisoned in a painful place,
being in the favour of your local gods,

(even as) you shall say, "An offering-that-the-king-gives to
   Osiris, lord of Abydos,
the great god Wennefer:
a thousand of bread and beer,
flesh and fowl,
an invocation offering at every festival,
for the spirit of the Keeper of the Diadem, the liegeman of the
   Great House,
Nebipusenwosret, begotten of Ita."
(This is) breath of the mouth,
excellent for the noble dead!
It is nothing wearisome.
You shall be an imperishable star,
a star in She-of-a-thousand-(shining)-souls.'

55–7 Letters to the dead

55 To a beloved wife

In 1958 an Egyptologist saw a stela, about 30 cm tall, which has since disappeared without
trace into the art market. It showed a scene of a man making offerings, and on the back,
known only from the scholar's hasty copy, was a letter in hieratic. The stela probably dated
from the 10th Dynasty and came from a tomb chapel, perhaps at Nag' el-Deir. In the letter
Merirtifi greets his dead wife and asks her to intercede for him; he promises to look after and
increase her mortuary cult in return for a message in a dream, during his vigil in the tomb.
Her brother makes a similar request.

A message from Merirtifi to Nebitef:
'How are you? Is the west taking care (of you) [as you] desire?
Look, I am your beloved on earth,
(so) fight for me, intercede for my name!
I have not garbled a spell before you, while making your name
   to live upon earth.[1]
Drive off the illness of my limbs!
May you appear for me as a blessed one before me,
that I may see you fighting for me in a dream.
I shall lay down offerings for you when the sun's light has
   risen,
and I shall establish an altar for you.'
A message from Khuau to his sister:
'[.....] I have not garbled a spell before you; I have not taken
   offerings away from you.
Now, I have sought [your benefit(?)]. Fight for me!
Fight for my wife and my children!'

---

[1] i.e., I have performed your funerary cult without any error.

142

56 To an unhelpful husband

The letter is written on the inside and then the outside of a rough, red pottery bowl 40 cm in diameter, now in the Cairo Museum. It was probably found at Saqqara, and the text dates from the early 12th Dynasty. Dedi writes to her dead husband, curtly reminding him that the mainstay of their house, the serving-girl, is ill. As the illness is thought to be the result of hostile spirits, she tells her husband to ward off these ghosts and appeals to his desire for the family's well-being and for his own funerary libations. The bowl would have been placed in her husband's tomb with a food offering inside it.

> Sent by Dedi to the priest Intef,
> born of Iunakht:
> As for this serving-maid Imiu who is ill
> – can you not fight for her day and night
> with any man who is doing her harm, and any woman who is
>   doing her harm?
> Why do you want your threshold to be made desolate?
> Fight for her again – now! –
> so that her household may be re-established and libations
>   poured for you.
> If there's no help from you, your house'll be destroyed;
> don't you know that it's this serving-maid who makes your
>   house amongst men?
> Fight for her! Watch over her!
> Save her from all those doing her harm!
> Then your house and your children shall be established. Good
>   be your hearing!

outside   inside

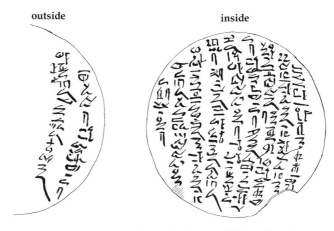

The Cairo bowl (DIAM. 40 cm; from Gardiner and Sethe, *Egyptian Letters to the Dead*, pl.6).

57 A denial of murder

Meru was an overseer of priests at Nag' el-Deir in the 10th Dynasty, and this letter (24 × 8 cm) was found folded in the tomb courtyard, having been placed either in Meru's tomb or in a

A scene from the west wall of the tomb of Meru at Nag' el-Deir, showing Meru (a), his son (b) and the servant Seni (c); H. *c.* 210 cm.

subsidiary burial in the courtyard, belonging to a relative who would have delivered the letter to the dead man. The letter is written by his son Heni, also a priest. Alarmed by a dream in which he saw his father with a dead servant called Seni, he writes denying responsibility for 'what happened' to this Seni – presumably death. A scene on the west wall of Meru's tomb shows the *dramatis personae* in idealised form, far from the murderous acts alluded to here.

> (Address:) The Patrician and Count,
> Overseer of Priests, Meru.
> (from)   Heni

> A servant speaks before his lord;
> [his son] Heni says:
> 'Attention a million times!
> Excellent is (giving) attention to him who makes (funerary)
>   provision for you,
> about these things which your servant Seni has done,
> and to this humble servant's[1] being made to see him (Seni)
> in a dream, in the same city as you.
> For, look, it was his character which carried himself off.

[1] i.e., the sender of the letter, Heni.

144

For, look, the things which happened to him could not have
    happened
through the action of this humble servant –
that (action) wasn't the sum of all that happened.
For, look, it wasn't I who har[med him]. Others did it before
    this humble servant.[1]
Pray, may his[1] lord be protective, may he be not evil-minded,
may one beware of him, until he has failed to watch this
    humble servant, for eternity![2]

58 Death and mutability: the 'Harpist's Song'

The song is preserved in a fragment of an 18th-Dynasty tomb and among a Ramessid collection of love lyrics. According to the title the original was carved in the mortuary chapel of a King Intef, beside a representation of a harpist (compare **40, 47**). This king is probably one of the rulers of the 11th Dynasty buried at Thebes, perhaps Wahankh Intef (II), whose chapel with the 'Dog stela' (**39a**), was accessible in the Ramessid period.

   The song is associated with the funerary celebrations by its title; like **50** it presents a brutal contrast between the losses and the benefit caused by death. The opening verses allude to the well-being of the dead man, but the harpist moves to evoke the impermanence of funerary provisions. In the central stanza this doubt is developed: even the sages of the Old Kingdom have no monuments left. In the last verse the singer urges carefreeness, with phrases which present this as the only appropriate funeral preparation. In the mixture of tones a balance between despair and hope, the endurance and decay of the dead, is achieved.

The Song which is in the chapel of Intef, true of voice,
which is before the singer with the harp:

This great one is well!
Good is the destiny, good the destruction!
For a generation passes,
and another remains, since the time of the ancestors,
those gods who existed aforetime,
who rest in their pyramids,
and the blessed noble dead likewise,
buried in their pyramids.
The builders of chapels, their places are no more.
What has become of them?

I have heard the words of Imhotep and Hordedef,
whose sayings are so told:
what of their places? Their walls have fallen;
their places are no more, like those who never were.
None returns from there to tell their conditions,
to tell their state, to reassure us,
until we attain the place where they have gone.

---

[2] i.e., beware of Seni, until he has stopped haunting me in dreams. The 'watching' may allude to the
  evil eye.

May you be happy with this, forgetfulness giving you
  benediction.
Follow your heart while you live!
Put myrrh on your head!
Clothe yourself with fine linen!
Anoint yourself with true wonders of the divine rite!
Increase your happiness!
Be not weary-hearted! Follow your heart and happiness!
Make your things on earth! Do not destroy your heart,
until that day of lamentation comes for you!
The Weary-hearted does not hear their lamentation;
mourning cannot save a man from the tomb-pit.

CHORUS: Make holiday! Do not weary of it!
Look, no one can take his things with him.
Look, no one who has gone there returns again.

Epilogue

Despite devouring time and the realisation that funerary rituals did not
endure, the written word offered the Egyptians some hope of permanence.
The New Kingdom scribes saw in the preservation of ancient texts an image
of the immortality mankind desired. The writing, whose development had
been shaped by a funerary context, itself performed the beatification which it
was intended merely to assist, and performs it still. Through texts the names
of the ancient dead are still recited upon earth.

59 Visitors' graffiti: from the tomb of Intefiqer's mother

The vizier Intefiqer has featured in several documents (**22, 27, 31, 46, 47**). His mother's tomb
on the west bank at Thebes was visited by groups of scribes of the early 18th Dynasty, who
left tourist graffiti on the 400-year-old walls of its entrance passageway (see **22**). The tomb
was already exposed then, abandoned and robbed, much as it is now.

The visitors obviously misread some of the texts: Im[...] and Bak thought the tomb dated
to the reign of Queen Sobekneferu (1760–1756 BC), having been mislead by the similar name
of Intefiqer's wife (Satsasobek) who was portrayed on the tomb walls (**59a, 59b**). Although
their inability to read the painted hieroglyphs is paralleled in the slips they made in their
own writing, they were not unusually incompetent: a similar but more serious error was
made by visitors to a nomarch's tomb at Beni Hasan (ancient Menat-*Khufu*), which they
identified as a rock-cut temple of King Khufu of the 4th Dynasty (see n.1).

Amenemhat, an official of Tuthmosis III (1479–1426 BC), made an error repeated by the
modern excavators thirty-three centuries later: he attributed the tomb to the vizier himself
(**59d**). His admiration was nonetheless sincere: he had his tomb carved just round the corner
of the hill, and modelled some of its scenes on those he had seen here.

As we now know, Intefiqer had fallen from favour, and these graffiti are poignantly, if
unwittingly, ironic: the texts and paintings have preserved the memory even of one whom
the State wanted forgotten.

59a

> The scribe Im[... son of(?) ...] came
> to see this tomb [of Sobekneferu]
> with ‹his› friend Hotep [.....].

59b

> The scribe Bak ‹came›
> to see ‹this› tomb ‹of› the time of Sobekneferu.
> He found it like heaven in its interior.[1]

---

[1] A fuller version of this style of graffiti, from Beni Hasan, continues:
> 'with the sun shining in it;
> ‹and he said, "May heaven rain fresh myrrh›
> and sprinkle incense
> upon this temple of that Khufu, true of voice." '

59c

> The scribe Djehuti, true of voice, came
> to see this tomb of the time of Kheperkare – may he live for all
>   time.
> And then he praised god greatly (for it).

The tourist graffito of Djehuti (from Davies-Gardiner, *Antefoqer*, pl.37, no.29).

59d

> The scribe Amenemhat,
> son of the Elder of the Portal Djehutimes,
> who was born of Intef, came
> to see [this] tomb [of the Lord Vizier] Intefiqer.
> It was pleasant to his heart [....]
> [....a monument(?)] which exists,
> excellent for all time.
> His name shall exist [for eternity....]
> [...with] offerings in it,
> saying: 'An offering-which-the-king-gives to Osiris [Foremost
>   of the Westerners],
> [and Amen]-Re, and the gods who are lords of the necropolis:
> invocation offerings of bread and beer,
> flesh and fowl,
> alabaster and linen,
> incense and unguent,
> all the goodly pure things,
> which heaven gives, and earth creates,
> and the inundation brings, as his offering
> to the spirit of Intefiqer, true of voice!'

60 The endurance of writing: a eulogy to dead authors

There are many miscellanies of short literary texts from the late New Kingdom which contain prayers, letters and praises of scribedom. These stanzas come from a 19th-Dynasty papyrus, some 2.5 m long; on the recto is a series of hymns, and on the verso a set of didactic maxims, including this eulogy of writers. As in **58**, the decay of tombs is evoked, but here writing offers an escape from mutability. This is compatible with statements elsewhere in wisdom literature that virtue is the only means of endurance, since writing, as the preserver of information, is synonymous with ancient wisdom, and wisdom with virtue. Time has confirmed the scribe's claim and many of the sages' works survive still (see glossary; and **2, 15, 17**).

These stanzas are followed by further injunctions to become a scribe, with warnings against thinking that 'ignorant and learned are alike'. This section of the miscellany concludes with an invocation to Khety, the master scribe and author of **9, 17**.

60a

But, should you do these things, you are wise in writings.
As for those scribes and sages
from the time which came after the gods
– those who would foresee what was to come, which
    happened –
their names endure for eternity,
although they are gone, although they completed their
    lifetimes and all their people are forgotten.

They did not make pyramids of bronze,
with stelae of iron.
They recognised not how heirs last as children,
with [offspring] pronouncing their names;
they made for themselves heirs
as writings and the Teachings they made.

They appointed [for themselves] the book as the lector-priest,
the writing board as Beloved-Son,
the Teachings as their pyramids,
the pen as their baby,
the stone-surface as wife.
From the great to the small
are given to be his children:
the scribe, he is their head.

Doors and mansions were made: they have fallen,
their funerary priests leaving,
while their stelae are covered with earth,
their chambers forgotten.
(Yet) their names are (still) pronounced over their rolls
which they made, from when they were.
How good is the memory of them and what they made –
for the bounds of eternity!

Be a scribe! Put it in your heart,
that your name shall exist like theirs!
The roll is more excellent than the carved stela,
than the enclosure which is established.
These act as chapels and pyramids
in the heart of him who pronounces their names.
Surely a name in mankind's mouth
is efficacious in the necropolis!

A man has perished: his corpse is dust,
and his people have passed from the land;
it is a book which makes him remembered
in the mouth of a speaker.
More excellent is a roll than a built house,
than a chapel in the west.
It is better than an established villa,
than a stela in a temple.

Is there any here like Hordedef?
Is there another like Imhotep?
There is none among our people like Nefer‹t›i,
or Khety their chief.
I shall make you know the name of Ptahemdjehuty and
    Khakheperresonbe.
Is there another like Ptahhotep,
or likewise, Kaires?

These sages, who foretold what comes –
what came from their mouths happened –
one benefits from the lines
written in their books.
To them the offspring of others are given,
to be heirs as if their own children.
They hid from the masses their magic,
which is read from their Teachings.
Departing life has made their names forgotten;
it is writings which make them remembered.

60b

[Repeating] life, the sight of the sun to the scribe Khety!
Invocation offerings of bread and beer before Wennefer,
cool water, wine and linen
to his spirit and his company – he whose lines are choice!
I shall give out his name for eternity; it was he who made the
    book
of the 'Teaching of the Dual King: Sehotepibre l.p.h.',
when he was at rest, united with the sky,
and entered among the lords of the necropolis.
These [matters(?)], he made [them(?)] endure […],
[.......] beside Sehotepibre l.p.h.
[..... ....] content,
[while(?)] the generations who come into being [pass by].
So let a man, as one who is educated, speak
[a blessing(?)] in front of the [scribe Khe]ty, true of voice!

Glossary

Aawoserre The fifth(?) Hyksos ruler of the 15th Dynasty, also named Apep.

Abydos A cult centre of Osiris Foremost of the Westerners, and Wepwawet. Osiris was supposedly buried in the necropolis, giving it particular sanctity.

Akhet The first of the three seasons of the Egyptian year, the 'inundation'. It was both a four-month period of the civil calendar and a season of the natural year. The two rarely correlated, and in dates Akhet refers to the season of the civil calendar.

Amen/Amen-Re The god of Thebes.

Anubis The jackal-headed god of embalming.

aroura A measure of land, ⅔ acre or 2,735 square m.

Atum The 'Undifferentiated one', the god of the primeval time and creation.

Bark of Millions The bark of the sun god, in which he traverses sky and Netherworld.

Bauefre A son of King Khufu, mentioned in several Middle Kingdom texts. There is no evidence that he succeeded as king.

Beloved-Son A funerary priest who acts as the deceased's son – as Horus did for Osiris – in the ritual of burial and beatification.

block statue A statue showing a person squatting so that only head, arms and feet are shown, protruding out of the block of stone.

Busiris A cult centre of Osiris in the delta.

cenotaph A funerary chapel, particularly at Abydos; see **53**.

deben The standard unit of weight (and value), equal to 91 g.

Determinative A sign (taxogram) at the end of a word, indicating its class or area of meaning.

Dual King A title, literally 'He-of-the-Sedge, He-of-the-Bee', which refers to two aspects of the kingship (once thought to have geographical reference: 'King of Upper and Lower Egypt'). It introduces the royal prenomen (throne-name).

Duamutef One of the four sons of Horus.

Elephantine The southernmost town of Egypt, close to the first cataract.

ennead The company of gods.

Foremost of the Westerners The ruler of the dead, and god of the necropolis at Abydos. An epithet of Osiris.

gallon (*heqat*) A measure of grain, equal to 4.54 litres; 16 gallons make up 1 sack.

Geb The earth god and father of Osiris.

Gold An epithet of Hathor.

Golden Horus The third element of the royal fivefold titulary. It refers to the king as Horus.

Hapy One of the four sons of Horus.

Hathor A benevolent solar goddess, with maternal and fertile aspects, who was connected with rebirth and foreign lands. In her hostile aspect she was Sekhmet.

Harakhti 'Horus of the Horizon', a solar god.

Heliopolitan nome The province of On/Heliopolis.

Heracleopolis The capital of the 9th-10th Dynasties. In mythology it is associated with Osiris, and in particular with his coronation and vindication.

Herwer Modern Hur, a town north of Hermopolis; a cult centre of two gods who were associated with birth.

Hordedef A prince of King Khufu, who died before ascending the throne. A teaching which was attributed to him survives, and he is portrayed in the 'Tales from the Court of Khufu' of Papyrus Westcar.

Horus The falcon god of the sky, and the royal god; he was also the son and vindicator of Osiris. As such 'Horus' was used as an elevated designation of the king, and was a royal title, the first element of the king's titulary.

Imhotep An official of King Djoser's (3rd Dynasty: 2630–2611 BC), who was regarded in subsequent periods as the supreme sage, and eventually deified.

Imsety One of the four sons of Horus.

Isis A royal goddess, the dutiful wife of Osiris, who assists in his resurrection by their son Horus.

Itj-tawi 'The Seizer of the Two Lands', the capital of the 12th Dynasty, near Memphis.

Kaires An Old Kingdom sage, who may be the supposed author of the fragmentary 'Instruction for Kagemni', which is preserved in the 12th-Dynasty Papyrus Prisse, and set in the 4th Dynasty.

Khafre A ruler of the 4th Dynasty and the builder of the second pyramid at Giza.

Khakheperre The prenomen (throne-name) of Senwosret II.

Khakheperresonbe The author of a surviving 'Lament'. His name ('Khakheperre-is-well') suggests a date under Senwosret II or later.

Kheperkare The prenomen (throne-name) of Senwosret I.

Khepri 'Becoming': the god of creation and the rising sun.

Kheraha An important religious centre, near modern 'Old Cairo'. In myths, associated with Horus' fight against Seth.

Khufu A ruler of the 4th Dynasty and the builder of the Great Pyramid. He is portrayed in later literature as ruthless.

lector-priest The priest who recites the texts in religious, funerary and magical rituals. In texts it is a prestigious office, synonymous with wisdom.

Letopolis A Delta town, north-west of Cairo. The local god was Horus.

Life of the Two Lands A name for Memphis, alluding to its position at the junction of Upper and Lower Egypt.

Lord of the Hand The creator god. The epithet may refer to him as a lord of action or to his having created the world through masturbation.

Lord (and Lady) to the Limit An epithet of the omnipotent creator god, which is also applied to the king (and queen).

l.p.h. 'Life, prosperity and health!', an invocation of well-being for superiors, especially the king, which was written after their names in abbreviated form.

Magic The personification of magical power, and a companion of the creator.

Medjai The nomads of the eastern deserts of Nubia (the so-called 'Pan grave people').

Memphis The capital during the Old Kingdom.

Menats Ceremonial necklaces, sacred to Hathor.

Meskhenet The goddess of good fortune.

Min The ithyphallic god of fertility.

Montu A Theban god.

Nag' el-Deir A town in Upper Egypt, near modern Girga.

Nekhbet A protectress of the king, 'She of Hierakonpolis'.

Nekhen Modern Kom el-Ahmar, known to the Greeks as Hierakonpolis. It was a pre-dynastic capital, which retained its association with the king in later symbolism and myth.

Nepri The god of corn.

Nimaatre The prenomen (throne-name) of Amenemhat III.

nomes The 'provinces' of Egypt, which was divided into twenty-two Upper Egyptian and twenty Lower Egyptian nomes, each with a governor (**nomarch**). Much of the period's history reflects the tension between their provincial independence and their role as parts of the central administration.

Nut The sky goddess, mother of Osiris and his siblings.

an offering-which-the-king-gives A funerary offering rite. The phrase, to be recited for the dead, invokes a royal offering to various gods, who will ensure the deceased's benefit from it. This reflects the actual practice of temple offerings being redistributed to private cults.

On The solar cult centre, called Heliopolis by the Greeks, now largely destroyed under a suburb of modern Cairo.

onomasticon An encyclopaedic list of words (see 18).

Osiris The god of the dead. Myths recounted how he ruled Egypt, was murdered by Seth, and resurrected and vindicated by his wife and son. He was the pattern for all the men who in death become assimilated with him as the 'Osiris N'.

ostracon A flake of limestone used as a convenient, if usually rather small, writing surface. Ostraca are particularly associated with the New Kingdom village of Deir el-Medineh and with scribal exercises written there.

Pe Modern Tell el-Fara'in, known to the Greeks as Buto; a sacred town-site of Lower Egypt.

Peace-of-Senwosret-true-of-voice The town founded by Senwosret II at modern el-Lahun (see 28).

Perception A personification, associated with the creator god's intellect; also a quality of the king.

Peret The second season of the year: 'winter', when the fields emerge (*per*) from the inundation (see Akhet).

Power-of-Senwosret-true-of-voice The pyramid complex of Senwosret II at modern el-Lahun (see 28).

Ptah The creator god of Memphis.

Ptahemdjehuti An otherwise unknown sage, who was perhaps supposed to have lived in the Middle Kingdom.

Qebhsenuf A son of Horus.

Rapacity Apparently a primordial monster, whose subduing was part of creation.

Re The god of the sun, the creator.

recto The front of a roll or sheet of papyrus.

Redjedef The successor of King Khufu, married to one of his daughters.

Re-Harakhti The god of the rising sun (a compound of Re and Horus-of-the-horizon).
Rennenet 'She who nourishes', the goddess of good fortune and destiny.
Reporter An official in the State administration.
Residence The capital, the royal residence at Itj-tawi.
Restau The desert of the Memphite necropolis, sacred to Sokar, the god of death. The name means 'the place of dragging (the hearse to the tomb)', and can also refer to the kingdom of Sokar in the Netherworld.
ro 1/320 gallon, equal to 14.2 ml.

Sehotepibre The prenomen (throne-name) of Amenemhat I.
Sekhemkare The prenomen (throne-name) of Amenemhat V, the fourth king of the 13th Dynasty.
Sekhmet The lioness goddess, a fierce solar deity, the protectress of the world and lady of plague. In her benevolent aspect she is associated with Hathor.
Selqet The scorpion goddess.
Seth The brother and assassin of Osiris, and rival of Horus. The god of confusion.
Shemu The third season of the year: the hot, 'dry' season (see Akhet).
She-of-a-thousand-(shining)-souls A name for the starry night sky.
Shu The god of air and sunlight. He was the son of the creator and grandfather of Osiris.
Sile Modern Tell Abu Sefa, a border town on the north-east edge of the delta.
Sistra Musical instruments similar to the rattle, sacred to Hathor.
Sobek The crocodile god, the ferocious lord of the waters.
Sokhet The goddess of the marshlands.
Son of Re A title of the king, prefacing the nomen (birth-name), and alluding to his descent from divinity.
Sopdu, Lord of the East The god worshipped at el-Lahun. He was a falcon god associated (like Hathor) with foreign lands.
Sothis The Dog-star, whose heliacal rising marked the start of the inundation. As the civil year was not fixed to the natural year, the date of this rising varied, and records of it provide us with vital chronological information.
Southern City Thebes
sunfolk Both a mythological group of beings associated with the sun and a term for all humanity who live under the sun.

Tayet The goddess of weaving.
Tefnut The divine sister of Shu.
Tenenet A sanctuary of the god of the dead at Memphis.
Thinis Modern Girga, the capital of the province containing Abydos.
Thoth The ibis-god of writing and wisdom; the god of Hermopolis, capital of the 15th Upper Egyptian nome.
Tjebu Modern Qaw el-Kebir.
true of voice An epithet referring to justification in judgement after death, thus marking the person as 'deceased'. Occasionally it can refer to a living person (e.g., **59c**); in later manuscripts it is often added, although not present in the original (e.g., in **5**).
Two Banks Egypt (the two strips of land on either side of the Nile).
Two Ladies The patron goddesses of Upper and Lower Egypt, who appear on the royal diadem. It is a royal title, introducing the second element of the titulary.
Two Lands See Two Banks.

Utterance A personification of the sun god's creative Word. He was often associated with Perception.

verso The back of a roll or sheet of papyrus.

Wag festival A festival commemorating the vindi-cation of Osiris, on the 17th–18th day of month 1 of Akhet. It was a 'night of the dead' when offerings were made to all the blessed dead.
the Weary-hearted An epithet of the dead Osiris.
Wennefer An epithet of Osiris, 'Perfect Being'.
Wepwawet A jackal-god, who 'Opens the ways', especially the ways to the Netherworld for Osiris at Abydos.

Bibliography

Abbreviations

The abbreviations are those of W. Helck *et al.* (ed.), *Lexicon der Ägyptologie*, vols I-VII, Wiesbaden: Otto Harrassowitz, 1975–.

ÄA	Ägyptologische Abhandlungen, Wiesbaden
AHAW	Abhandlungen der Heidelberger Akademie der Wissenschaften, Phil.-hist. Kl., Heidelberg
ANOC	Abydos North Offering Chapel
AO	Der Alte Orient, Leipzig
APAW	Abhandlungen der Preussischen Akademie der Wissenschaften, Berlin, from 1945: ADAW
ASE	Archaeological Survey Of Egypt, London.
AV	Archäologische Veröffentlichungen, Deutsches Archäologisches Institut, Abt. Cairo, Vol. 1–3 Berlin, Vol. 4ff. Mainz
BAe	Bibliotheca Aegyptiaca, Brussels
BdE	Bibliothèque d'étude, Institut français d'archéologie orientale, Cairo
BSEG	*Bulletin de la Société d'egyptologie de Genève*, Geneva
BSFE	*Bulletin de la Société française d'égyptologie*, Paris
CdE	*Chronique d'Égypte*, Brussels
DE	*Discussions in Egyptology*, Oxford
EEF	Egypt Exploration Fund, London
EES	Egypt Exploration Society, London
GM	*Göttinger Miszellen*, Göttingen
HÄB	Hildesheimer Ägyptologische Beiträge, Hildesheim
IFAO	L'institut français d'archéologie orientale, Cairo
JAOS	*Journal of the American Oriental Society*, New Haven
JARCE	*Journal of the American Research Center in Egypt*, Boston
JEA	*Journal of Egyptian Archaeology*, London
JNES	*Journal of Near Eastern Studies*, Chicago
KÄT	Kleine Ägyptische Texte, Wiesbaden
LÄ	Lexikon der Ägyptologie, Wiesbaden
MAN	*Man. A Monthly Record of Anthropological Science*, London
MÄS	Münchner Ägyptologische Studien, Berlin, Munich
MDAIK	*Mitteilungen des Deutschen Archaologischen Instituts, Abteilung Kairo*; until 1944: Mitteilungen des Deutschen Instituts für Ägyptische Altertumskunde in Kairo, Berlin, Wiesbaden, from 1970: Mainz
MFA	Museum of Fine Arts, Boston
MMJ	*Metropolitan Museum Journal*, New York
NISABA	Religious Texts Translation Series, NISABA, Leiden
OBO	Orbis Biblicus et Orientalis, Fribourg
OLZ	*Orientalistische Literaturzeitung*, Berlin, Leipzig
Or	*Orientalia*, Nova Series, Rome
PMMA	Publications of the Metropolitan Museum of Art, Egyptian Expedition, New York
RdE	*Revue d'égyptologie*, Cairo; from vol. 7: Paris
RIDA	*Revue internationale des droits de l'antiquité*, 3éme série, Brussels
SAK	*Studien zur Altägyptischen Kultur*, Hamburg
SSEA	*Society of the Studies of Egyptian Antiquities*, Toronto
TÄB	Tübinger Ägyptologische Beiträge, Bonn
TTS	The Theban Tombs Series, London
UGAÄ	Untersuchungen zur Geschichte und Altertumskunde Ägyptens, Leipzig, Berlin
WdO	*Die Welt des Orients*. Wissenchaftl. Beiträge zur Kunde des Morgenlandes, Wuppertal: 1949: Stuttgart; from 1954: Göttingen
ZÄS	*Zeitschrift für Ägyptische Sprache und Altertumskunde*, Leipzig, Berlin

Introduction

The historical setting
J. Baines and J. Málek, *Atlas of Ancient Egypt*. Oxford: Phaidon Press, 1980.
The best guide to the material remains of the period is:
J. Bourriau, *Pharaohs and Mortals: Egyptian Art in the Middle Kingdom* [exhibition catalogue]. Cambridge: Cambridge University Press, 1988.
An excellent introduction to the workings of Egyptian culture is:
B. Kemp, *Ancient Egypt: Anatomy of a Civilization*. London and New York: Routledge, 1989.
The chronology for the Middle Kingdom is that of:
R. Krauss, *Sothis- und Monddaten: Studien zur astronomischen und technischen Chronologie Altägyptens*. HÄB 20, 1985.

The nature of the writings

The script and its development
J. Assmann, 'Schrift, Tod und Identität: das Grab als Vorschul der Literatur im alten Ägypten', in A. Assmann *et al.* (ed.), *Schrift und Gedächtnis: Beiträge zur Archäologie der literarischen Kommunikation*, 64–93. Munich: Fink, 1983.
W.V. Davies, *Egyptian Hieroglyphs*. London: British Museum Publications, 1987.
G. Posener, 'Sur l'emploi de l'encre rouge dans les manuscrits égyptiens', *JEA* 37 (1951), 75–80.

A survey of the uses of writing
J. Assmann, 'Der literarische Text im alten Ägypten: Versuch einer Begriffbestimmung', *OLZ* 69 (1974), 117–26.
J. Baines, 'Literacy and Ancient Egyptian Society', *Man* 18 (1983), 572–99, with bibliography.
J. Baines and C.J. Eyre, 'Four Notes on Literacy', *GM* 61 (1983), 65–96.
F. Junge, 'Sprache', LÄ V (1984), 1176–1211.
W.J. Ong, *Orality and Literacy: the Technologizing of the World*. New Accents. London: Methuen, 1982.

The nature of the anthology
W.K. Simpson, 'Papyri of the Middle Kingdom,' in S. Sauneron (ed.), *Textes et langages de l'Egypte pharaonique* II, 63–72. BdE 64/2.

Technical note
G. Burkard, 'Der formale Aufbau altägyptischer Literatur: zur Problematik der Entschliessung seiner Grundstrukturen', *SAK* 10 (1983), 79–118.
G. Fecht, 'Prosodie', LÄ IV (1982), 1127–54.

The writings
References are given to the publications of each text and to commentaries (selective), and to discussions of points of detail where appropriate. For (full) translations of **1–3, 4–7, 9–10, 12–15, 17, 41, 43, 50, 51, 58** see M. Lichtheim, *Ancient Egyptian Literature: a Book of Readings I: the Old and Middle Kingdoms*. Berkeley: University of California Press, 1974.

1   Coffin Text Spells 1130 and 1031
A. de Buck, *The Ancient Egyptian Coffin Texts* VII, 461–71, 262. (University of Chicago Oriental Institute Publications 87.) Chicago: University of Chicago Press, 1961.
J. Assmann, *Ägypten: Theologie und Frömmigkeit einer frühen Hochkultur*, 204–8. Stuttgart: Kohlhammer, 1984.
G. Fecht, *Der Vorwurf an Gott in den 'Mahnworten des Ipu-wer'*, 120–7, AHAW 1972, 1.
L.H. Lesko, *The Ancient Egyptian Book of Two Ways*, 130–3. (University of California Publications, Near Eastern Studies 17.) Berkeley: University of California Press, 1972.

E. Otto, 'Zur Komposition von Coffin Texts Spell 1130,' in J. Assmann *et al.* (ed.), *Fragen an die altägyptische Literatur: Studien zum Gedenken an Eberhard Otto*, 1–18. Wiesbaden: Reichert, 1977.

2   Neferti 9a–12g
W. Helck, *Die Prophezeiung der Nfr.tj*, 34–47, KÄT 1970.
E. Blumenthal, 'Die Prophezeiung des Neferti', *ZÄS* 109 (1982), 1–27.
idem, 'Neferti, Prophezeiung des', LÄ IV (1982), 380–1.

3   Sinuhe B 147–73; AO recto 56–63
A.M. Blackman, *Middle Egyptian Stories*, 29–31, BAe 2, 1932.
J.W.B. Barns, *The Ashmolean Ostracon of Sinuhe*, 14–17, pl. [5]. London: Oxford University Press for Griffith Institute, 1952.
A.H. Gardiner, *Notes on the Story of Sinuhe*, 57–63. Paris: Champion, 1916.
M. Malaise, 'La Traduction de Sinouhé B 160', *GM* 10 (1974), 29–34.
W.K. Simpson, 'Sinuhe', LÄ V (1984), 950–5.
W. Westendorf, 'Sinuhe B 160', in W. Helck (ed.), *Festschrift für Siegfried Schott zu seinem 70. Geburtstag*, 125–31. Wiesbaden: Harrassowitz, 1968.
W. Westendorf, 'Einst-Jetzt-Einst, oder: Die Rückkehr zum Ursprung', *WdO* 17 (1986), 4–8.

4
J. Assmann, *Der König als Sonnenpriester: ein kosmographischer Begleittext zur kultischen Sonnenhymnik in thebanischer Tempeln und Gräbern*, ADAIK 7, 1970.

5
L. Stern, 'Urkunde über der Bau des Sonnentempel zu On', *ZÄS* 12 (1874), 85–96, pl. 1–2.
A. de Buck, 'The Building Inscription of the Berlin Leather Roll,' in *Studia Aegyptiaca* I, 48–57. Analecta Orientalia 17 (1938).
H. Goedicke, 'The Berlin Leather Roll (P Berlin 3029),' in W. Müller (ed.), *Festschrift zum 150jährigen Bestehen des Berliner Ägyptisches Museums*, 87–104. Staatliche Museen zu Berlin, Mitteilungen aus der ägyptischen Sammlung 8, (1974). Berlin: Akademie.
Sanaa Abd El-Azim El-Adly, 'Die Berliner Lederhandschrift (pBerlin 3029)', *WdO* 15 (1984), 6–18.
See also J. Osing, 'Königsnovelle', LÄ III (1980), 556–7.

6   Berlin Museum 1157
K. Sethe, *Ägyptische Lesestücke zum Gebrauch im akademischen Unterricht: Texte des Mittleren Reich*, 83–4. Leipzig: Hinrichs 1928.
W. Barta, 'Der Terminus *twt* auf den Grenzstelen

Sesostris' III in Nubia,' in W. Müller (ed.),
*Festschrift zum 150jährigen Bestehen des Berliner
Ägyptisches Museums*, 51–4. Staatliche Museen zu
Berlin, Mitteilungen aus der ägyptischen Sammlung
8 (1974). Berlin: Akademie.
W.V. Davies, '"Hands and hearts (Berlin 1157)" –
an alternative', *JEA* 62 (1976), 176–7.
J.M.A. Janssen, 'The Stela (Khartum Museum No.3)
from Uronarti', *JNES* 12 (1953), 51–5.
For the context of the fort see:
C.C. Van Siclen, *The Chapel of Sesostris III at
Uronarti*. San Antonio, Texas: published by author,
1982.

7   P. Kahun LV.1, (pl. 2) ll.11–20
F.Ll. Griffith, *The Petrie Papyri: Hieratic Papyri
from Kahun and Gurob*, pl. 2. London: Quaritch,
1898.
K. Sethe, *Ägyptische Lesestücke zum Gebrauch im
akademischen Unterricht: Texte des Mittleren
Reiches*, 67. Leipzig: Hinrichs, 1928.
H.Goedicke, 'Remarks on the Hymns to Sesostris
III', *JARCE* 7 (1968), 23–6.
M. Patanè, 'La structure de l'hymne a Sésostris III',
BSEG 8 (1983), 61–5.

8
E. Drioton, 'Une liste de rois de la IVe dynastie
dans l'Ouâdi Hammâmât,' *BSFE* 16 (1954), 41–9.
D.B. Redford, *Pharaonic king-lists, Annals and Day
Books: A Contribution to the Study of the Egyptian
Sense of History*, 25. SSEA Publications IV.
Mississauga, Ontario: Benben, 1986.

9
W. Helck, *Der Texte der 'Lehre Amenemhets I für
seinem Sohn,'* KÄT, 1969.
H. Goedicke, *Studies in 'the Instructions of King
Amenemhet I for his Son'* (Varia Aegyptiaca
Supplement 2). San Antonio: van Siclen Books,
1988; (Pt.1: commentary, Pt.2: plates).
E. Blumenthal, 'Die Lehre des Königs Amenemhet
(Teil I)', *ZÄS* 111 (1984), 85–107; Teil II, *ZÄS* 112
(1985), 104–15.
ibid., 'Lehre Amenemhets I', LÄ III (1980), 968–71.
G. Burkard, *Textkritische Untersuchungen zu
altägyptischen Weisheitslehren des Alten und
Mittleren Reiches*. ÄA 34, 1977.

10   Merikare 41a–47k
W. Helck, *Die Lehre für König Merikare*, 72–88,
KÄT, 1977.
J. Assmann, *Ägypten: Theologie und Frömmigkeit
einer frühen Hochkultur*, 201–4. Stuttgart:
Kohlhammer, 1984.
G. Posener, 'Lehre für Merikare,' LÄ III (1980), 986–9.

11
G. Posener, 'Le Conte de Néferkarè et du general

Siséné (Recherches littéraires IV)', *RdE* 11 (1957),
119–37.
E. Brunner-Traut, *Altägyptische Märchen*, 143–5,
283–4. Düsseldorf: Diederichs, 1963.
E. Richter-AerØe, 'Sisenet und Phiops II', LÄ V
(1984), 597.

12   Ipuur 13.9–14.4
A. Gardiner, *The Admonitions of an Egyptian Sage,
from a Hieratic Papyrus in Leiden*, 87–90, pl. 13–4.
Leipzig: Hinrichs, 1909.
G. Fecht, *Der Vorwurf an Gott in den 'Mahnworten
des Ipu–wer'*, AHAW 1972,1.
J. Spiegel, 'Admonitions,' LÄ I (1975), 65–6.

13   BM 581
*Hieroglyphic Texts from Egyptian Stelae, etc., in
the British Museum* II, pl. 23. London: British
Museum, 1912.
K. Sethe, *Ägyptische Lesestücke zum Gebrauch im
akademischen Unterricht: Texte des Mittleren
Reiches*, 80–1. Leipzig: Hinrichs, 1928.
W.K. Simpson, *The Terrace of The Great God at
Abydos: The Offering Chapels of Dynasties 12 and
13,* pl. 12 (ANOC 5.2). Publications of the
Pennsylvania-Yale Expedition to Egypt 5, 1974.
M. Lichtheim, *Ancient Egyptian Autobiographies
chiefly of the Middle Kingdom: A Study and an
Anthology*, 109–11, OBO 84, 1988.

14   Eloquent Peasant B1 289–326
F. Vogelsang, *Kommentar zu den Klagen des
Bauern*, 200–19, UGAÄ 6, 1913.
R.B. Parkinson, *The Tale of the Eloquent Peasant*,
40–6. Oxford: Griffith Institute, in press.
G. Fecht, 'Bauerngeschichte', LÄ I, 638–51, 1975.
A.H. Gardiner, 'The Eloquent Peasant', 19–20, *JEA*
9 (1923), 5–25.
R.B. Parkinson, *The Tale of the Eloquent Peasant;
A commentary*, 274–304. Oxford University,
doctoral thesis, 1988.
P. Vernus, Review of D. Silverman, *Interrogative
Constructions…*, 246, *CdE* 57/113–4 (1982), 243–9.

15   Ptahhotep (P) ll.42–59; 84–98; 186–96; 197–219;
220–31; 264–76; 277–97; 298–315; 325–38; 339–49
Z. Žába, *Les Maximes de Ptahhotep*. Prague:
Academie tchécoslovaque des sciences, 1956.
R. Caminos, *Literary Fragments in the Hieratic
Script*, pl. 28. Oxford University Press for Griffith
Institute, 1956.
H. Brunner, 'Lehre des Ptahhotep', LÄ III (1980),
990–9.
G. Burkard, *Textkritische Untersuchungen zu
ägyptischen Weisheitslehren des Alten und
Mittleren Reiches*, ÄA 34, 1977.
G. Fecht, *Der Habgierige und die Maat in der Lehre
des Ptahhotep (5. und 19. Maxime')*, ADAIK 1,
1958.

G. Fecht, 'Cruces Interpretum in der Lehre des Ptahhotep (Maximen 7, 9, 13, 14)', in [A. Guillamont (ed.)], *Hommages à François Daumas*, 227–51. Montpellier: Université de Montpellier, 1986.
P. Seibert, *Die Charakteristik: Untersuchungen zu einer altägyptischen Sprechsitte und ihren Ausprägungen in Folklore und Literatur. Teil I: Philologische Bearbweitung der Bezeugungen*, 72–7, ÄA 17, 1967.

16 Loyalist Teaching 9.1–14.12
G. Posener, *L'Enseignement loyaliste: sagesse égyptienne du Moyen Empire*, 109–39. (Centre de recherches d'histoire et de philologie II – Hautes études orientales 5.) Geneva: Droz, 1976.
G. Posener, 'Lehre, loyalistische', LÄ III (1980), 982–3.

17 The Satire on Trades 1a–4c, 7a–e, 12a–13c, 19a–23a, 28a–f, 30a–g
W. Helck, *Die Lehre des Dw3-Ḥtjj*, KÄT, 1970.
H. Brunner, 'Lehre des Cheti', LÄ III (1980), 977–8.
P. Seibert, *Die Charakteristik: Untersuchungen zu einer altägyptischen Sprechsitte und ihren Ausprägungen in Folklore und Literatur. Teil I: Philologische Bearbweitung der Bezeugungen*, 99–192, ÄA 17, 1967.

18 P Ramesseum D, P Berlin 10495
A.H. Gardiner, *Ancient Egyptian Onomastica, passim*, 6–23, pl. 1–5. London: Oxford University Press, 1947.
For identifications of the plants see:
G. Charpentier, *Receuil de matériaux épigraphiques relatifs à la botanique de l'Egypte antique*. Paris: Trismégiste, 1981.

19 P Rhind, problem 66
A.B. Chace *et al.*, *The Rhind Mathematical Papyrus II: Photographs, Transcription, Transliteration, Literal Translation*, pl. 1, 88. Oberlin, Ohio: Mathematical Association of America, 1929.
G. Robins and C. Shute, *The Rhind Mathematical Papyrus: an ancient Egyptian Text*. London: British Museum Publications, 1987.

20 P Kahun VI.1, 1.5–12 (nos.2–3)
F.Ll. Griffith, *The Petrie Papyri: Hieratic Papyri from Kahun and Gurob*, 5–7, pl. 5. London: Quaritch, 1898.
H. Grapow, *Die Medizinischen Texte in Hieroglyphischer Umschreibung Autographiert*, 458–9. (Grundriss der Medizin der alten Ägypter 5.) Berlin: Akademie, 1958.
H. von Dienes, H. Grapow and W. Westendorf, *Übersetzung der Medezinischen Texte*, 267. (Grundriss der Medezin der alten Ägypter 4.1.) Berlin: Akademie, 1958.

21
A.M. Blackman, *The Rock Tombs of Meir I: The Tomb Chapel of Ukh-Hotep's Son Senbi*, 22–7, pl. 2–3, ASE 22, 1914.

22
N. de G. Davies and A.H. Gardiner, *The Tomb of Antefoker, Vizier of Sesostris I, and of his Wife, Senet (No. 60)*, 15–16, pl. 11, TTS 2, 1920.
W. Guglielmi, *Reden, Rufe und Lieder auf altägyptischen Darstellungen der Landwirtschaft, Viehzucht, des Fisch- und Vogelsfangs vom Mittleren Reich bis zur Spätzeit*, 85–6, TÄB 1, 1973.

23
A.M. Blackman, *The Rock Tombs of Meir I: The Tomb Chapel of Ukh-Hotep's Son Senbi*, 29, pl. 3, ASE 22, 1914.
W. Guglielmi, *ibid.*, 54–5.

24
P.E. Newberry, *El Bersheh I: The tomb of Tehuti-hetep*, 31, pl. 22, ASE 3 [1892].
W. Guglielmi, *ibid.*, 173–4.

25 The Pleasures of Fishing and Fowling B.4.2–9
R. Caminos, *Literary Fragments in the Hieratic Script*, 14–16; pl. 3. Oxford: Oxford University Press for Griffith Institute, 1956.
The figure is from:
A.M. Blackman, *The Rock Tombs of Meir I: The Tomb Chapel of Ukh-Hotep's Son Senbi*, pl. 2, ASE 22, 1914.

26 Papyrus Brooklyn 35.1446, Insert C
W.C. Hayes, *A Papyrus of the Late Middle Kingdom in the Brooklyn Museum*, 71–85, pl. 6. Brooklyn: Brooklyn Museum, 1955.
W. Helck, *Historische-biographische Texte der 2. Zwischenzeit und neue Texte der 18. dynastie*, 11, KÄT, 1975.

27 P. Reisner II, sections D-F
W.K. Simpson, *Papyrus Reisner II: Accounts of the Dockyard Workshop at Thinis in the Reign of Sesostris I, Transcription and Commentary*, 20–3, 30, pl. 7–9. Boston: MFA, 1965.
G. Posener, 'Le Vizir Antefoqer', in J. Baines *et al.* (ed.) *Pyramid Studies and Other Essays presented to I.E.S. Edwards*, 73–7. (Occasional Publications 7.) London: EES, 1988.

28a P Berlin 10003 AII.13–19
28b P Berlin 10012.18–21
28c P Berlin 10050, 1–5
G. Möller, *Hieratische Lesestücke für den akademischen Gebrauch I: alt- und mittelhieratische Texte*, 18–19. Leipzig: Hinrichs, 1927.
K. Sethe, *Ägyptische Lesestücke zum Gebrauch im*

akademischen Unterricht: Texte des Mittleren Reiches, 96–7. Leipzig: Hinrichs, 1928.
On the archives as a whole see:
U. Luft, 'Illahunstudien, I: Zu der Chronologie und den Beamten in den Briefen aus Illahun', *Oikumene* 3 (1982), 101–56.
S. Quirke, *The Administration of Egypt in the Late Middle Kingdom: The Hieratic Documents*, 155–73. New Malden: Sia, 1990.

29a P Berlin 10014
29b P Kahun 2.2
G. Möller, *Hieratische Paläographie: die ägyptische Buchschrift in ihrer Entwicklung von der fünften Dynastie bis zur römischen Kaiserzeit I: bis zum Beginn der achtzehnten Dynastie*, pl. 4 [**29a** only]. Leipzig: Hinrichs, 1909.
G. Möller, *Hieratische Lesestücke für den akademischen Gebrauch I: alt- und mittelhieratische Texte*, 18–19. Leipzig: Hinrichs, 1927.
K. Sethe, *Ägyptische Lesestücke zum Gebrauch im akademischen Unterricht: Texte des Mittleren Reiches*, 97. Leipzig: Hinrichs, 1928.
29c P Berlin 10025
U. Luft, 'Illahunstudien, II: Ein Verteidigungsbrief aus Illahun,' *Oikumene* 4 (1983), 121–79.
29d P Kahun VI.8
F.Ll. Griffith, *The Petrie Papyri: Hieratic Papyri from Kahun and Gurob*, 76–7, pl. 32. London: Quaritch, 1898.

30 Semna Despatch No. 4; Papyrus Ramesseum C, 3.7–4.5
P.C. Smither, 'The Semna Despatches', 8–9, pl. 3–4, *JEA* 31 (1945), 3–10, pl. 1–7.
J. Bourriau, *Pharaohs and Mortals: Egyptian Art in the Middle Kingdom* [exhibition catalogue], 79–80. Cambridge: Cambridge University Press, 1988.
S. Quirke, *The Administration of Egypt in the Late Middle Kingdom: The Hieratic Documents*, 191–3. New Malden: Sia, 1990.

31 Graffiti from the Czechoslovak Concession in Nubia, nos 53 (**31a**), 73 (**31b**), 56 (**31c**)
31a
Z. Žába, *The Rock Inscriptions of Lower Nubia (Czechoslovak Concession)*, 74–6, figs. 101–2. (Czechoslovak Institute of Egyptology in Prague and in Cairo Publications, 1.) Prague: Charles University of Prague, 1974.
31b
Z. Žába, *ibid.*, 98–109, figs. 150–5.
31c
Z. Žába, *ibid.*, 79–81, figs. 110–11.

32 Sinai Inscription 90, the Stela of Horurre
A.H. Gardiner, T.E. Peet & J. Černý, *The*

Inscriptions of Sinai, I, pl. 25a–6, II, 97–9. London: Oxford University Press, 1952–5.
K. Sethe, *Ägyptische Lesestücke zum Gebrauch im akademischen Unterricht: Texte des Mittleren Reiches*, 86. Leipzig: Hinrichs, 1928.
E. Iversen, 'The Inscription of Herwerre' at Serâbit-al-Kâdem,' in F. Junge (ed.), *Studien zu Sprache und Religion Ägyptens: zu Ehren von Wolfhart Westendorf*, 508–19. Göttingen, 1984. (The most recent discussion with bibliography.}
For the site in general:
R. Giveon, *The Stones of Sinai Speak*. Tokyo: Gakuseisha, 1978.

33 Papyrus Brooklyn 35.1446, recto ll. 57–8, 63–4
W.C. Hayes, *A Papyrus of the Late Middle Kingdom in the Brooklyn Museum, passim*, pl. 5–7. Brooklyn: Brooklyn Museum, 1955.
S. Quirke, 'State and Labour in the Middle Kingdom: A Reconsideration of the Term *ḫnrt*', *RdE* 39 (1988), 83–106.
S. Quirke, *The Administration of Egypt in the Late Middle Kingdom: The Hieratic Documents*, 127–40. New Malden: Sia, 1990.

34 Heqanakht Letters I-II
T.G.H. James, *The Heqanakhte Papers and other Early Middle Kingdom Documents*, 1–45, pl. 1–7, PMMA 19, 1962.
K. Baer, 'An Eleventh Dynasty Farmer's Letters to his Family', *JAOS* 83 (1963), 1–19.
H. Goedicke, *Studies in the Heqanakhte Papers, passim*, 38–76 (**34a**), 13–37 (**34b**). Baltimore: Halgo, 1984.

35 P British Museum 10549
T.G.H. James, *The Heqanakhte Papers and other Early Middle Kingdom Documents*, 89–92, pl. 24–5 (no. 16), PMMA, 1962.
J. Bourriau, *Pharaohs and Mortals: Egyptian Art in the Middle Kingdom* [exhibition catalogue], 78–9. Cambridge: Cambridge University Press, 1988.

36 P Kahun I.1
F.Ll. Griffith, *The Petrie Papyri: Hieratic Papyri from Kahun and Gurob*, 31–5, pl.12–13. London: Quaritch, 1898.
K. Sethe, *Ägyptische Lesestücke zum Gebrauch im akademischen Unterricht: Texte des Mittleren Reiches*, 90–1. Leipzig: Hinrichs, 1928.
A. Theodorides, 'La vente à crédit du *Pap. Kahoun I,2* et ses conséquences', *RIDA* 8 (1961), 41–76.
idem, 'La propriété et ses démembrements en droit pharaonique', 33–6, *RIDA* 24 (1977), 21–64.
For Ankhreni see:
D. Franke, *Personendaten aus dem Mittleren Reiches (20.–16. Jahrhundert v. Chr.): Dossiers 1–796*, 145, ÄA 41, 1984.

37 P Kahun II.1
F.L1. Griffith, *The Petrie Papyri: Hieratic Papyri from Kahun and Gurob*, 36–8, pl.13. London: Quaritch, 1898.
K. Sethe, *Ägyptische Lesestücke zum Gebrauch im akademischen Unterricht: Texte des Mittleren Reiches*, 91–2. Leipzig: Hinrichs, 1928.

38 P Kahun I.4 verso (**38a**), I.5 (**38b**), I.3 ll.1–8 (**38c**)
F.Ll. Griffith, *The Petrie Papyri: Hieratic Papyri from Kahun and Gurob*, pl.9. London: Quaritch, 1898.
B. Kemp, *Ancient Egypt: Anatomy of a Civilization*, 157–8. London and New York: Routledge, 1989.

39 Dogs' names; in the published corpus, nos. 20, 19, 21–4, 32, 26, 29, 63, 37, 36
J.M.A. Janssen, 'Über Hundenamen im pharaonischer Ägypten', *MDAIK* 16 (1958), 176–82.
H.G. Fischer, 'A Supplement to Janssen's List of Dogs' Names', *JEA* 47 (1961), 152–3.
idem, 'More Ancient Egyptian Names of Dogs and Other Animals', *MMJ* 12 (1977), 173–8.
For **39a** see also:
D. Arnold, *Gräber des Alten und Mittleren Reiches in El-Tarif*, 52–6, pl. 53, AV 17, 1976.
H. Fischer, 'Hundestęle', LÄ III, 81–2.
For **39h** see also:
Jean Capart, 'Un cercueil de chien du Moyen Empire', *ZÄS* 44 (1907), 131.

40
W.K. Simpson, *The Terrace of The Great God at Abydos: The Offering Chapels of Dynasties 12 and 13*, pl. 56 (ANOC 38.1–2). Publications of the Pennsylvania-Yale Expedition to Egypt 5, 1974.
W.A. Ward, 'Neferhotep and his Friends: A Glimpse of the Life of Ordinary Men', *JEA* 63 (1977), 63–6.

41 A composite text based on: Cairo 20498, Louvre C.30 and Sobekdedu's stela, BM 243, Ashmolean Museum: The Queen's College Loan 1109, Brussels 5300 (19th Dynasty), and others
K. Sethe, *Ägyptische Lesestücke zum Gebrauch im akademischen Unterricht: Texte des Mittleren Reiches*, 64–5. Leipzig: Hinrichs, 1928.
S. Hassan, *Hymnes réligieux du Moyen Empire*, 5–84. Cairo: IFAO, 1928.
W.K. Simpson, *The Terrace of The Great God at Abydos: The Offering Chapels of Dynasties 12 and 13*, pl. 84 (ANOC 62.1–2). Publications of the Pennsylvania-Yale Expedition to Egypt 5, 1974.
P.C. Smither and A.N. Dakin, 'Stelae in the Queen's College, Oxford', 157–9, *JEA* 25 (1939), 157–65.
M. Patanè, 'La structure poétique de la stèle C 30 du Musée du Louvre', *BSEG* 6 (1982), 77–82.

42 P Kahun VI.12
F.Ll. Griffith, *The Petrie Papyri: Hieratic Papyri from Kahun and Gurob*. 4, pl. 3. London: Quaritch, 1898.
J.G. Griffiths, *The Conflict of Horus and Seth: from Egyptian and Classical Sources*, 42. Liverpool: University Press, 1960.

43 Ipuur 10.13–11.7
A.H. Gardiner, *The Admonitions of an Egyptian Sage, from a Hieratic Papyrus in Leiden*, 75–7, pl. 10–1. Leipzig: Hinrichs, 1909.
G. Fecht, *Der Vorwurf an Gott in den 'Mahnworten des Ipu-wer'*, esp. 28–30, AHAW 1972,1.

44 The 'White Chapel', scene 22
P. Lacau and H. Chevrier, *Une Chapelle de Sésostris Ier à Karnak*, pl. 22. Cairo: IFAO, 1956 (text), 1969 (plates).
H. Kees, 'Die Weisse Kapelle Sesostris I. in Karnak und das Sedfest', *MDAIK* 16 (1958), 194–213.

45 P Ramesseum B, scene 33
K. Sethe, *Dramatische Texte zu altägyptischen Mysterienspielen II: Der Dramatische Ramesseumspapyrus, ein Spiel zur Thronbesteigung des Königs*, 211–13, pl. 9, 20, UGAÄ 10, 1928.
H. Altenmüller, 'Dramatischer Ramesseumspapyrus', LÄ I (1975), 1132–40.

46 Execration Figure (Cairo J.E. 63955)
G. Posener, *Cinq Figures d'Envoûtement, passim*, pl. 1, 4. BdE 101 (1987).

47
N. de G. Davies and A.H. Gardiner, *The Tomb of Antefoker, Vizier of Sesostris I, and of his Wife, Senet (No. 60)*, 23–4, pl. 29, TTS 2, 1920.

48 Cairo 20281
K. Sethe, *Ägyptische Lesestücke zum Gebrauch im akademischen Unterricht: Texte des Mittleren Reiches*, 62–3. Leipzig: Hinrichs, 1928.
H.O.Lange and H. Schäfer, *Grab- und Denksteine des Mittleren Reichs im Museum von Kairo*, I, 295–6, IV, pl. 20. Berlin: Reichsdruckerei, 1902.

49 P Berlin 3027, recto 2.2–7, 3.8–4.2
A. Erman, *Zaubersprüche für Mutter und Kind: aus dem Papyrus 3027 des Berliner Museums*, 38–40, 43–4. APAW 1901.
J.F. Borghouts, *Ancient Egyptian Magical Texts*, 42–3 (nos. 67-8). (Religious Texts Translation Series NISABA 9.) Leiden: Brill, 1978.
For the magical wands see:
H. Altenmüller, *Die Aptropaia und die Götter Mittelägyptens: Eine typologische und religionsgeschichtliche Untersuchung der*

sogenannten 'Zaubermesser' des Mittleren Reiches, 180–3. (University of Munich, dissertation.) 1965.
The drawing of the seal (Basle 803) is based on:
C. Sourdive, La Main dans l'Egypte pharaonique: recherches de morphologie structurale sur les objets égyptiens comportant une main, 466. Bern & Frankfurt-am-Main: Lang, 1984.
See also:
J.R. Ogdon, 'Studies in Ancient Egyptian Magical Thought, I: The Hand and the Seal', DE 1 (1985), 27–34.

50 Lebensmüder ll.56–68; 130–47
R.O. Faulkner, 'The Man who was Tired of Life', passim, JEA 42 (1956), 21–40.
W. Barta, Das Gespräch eines Mannes mit seinem BA (Papyrus Berlin 3024). MÄS 18, 1969.
H. Goedicke, The Report about the Dispute of a Man with his Ba (P. Berlin 3024), 123–9, 172–82. Baltimore: Johns Hopkins University Press, 1970.

51 Sinuhe B 188–97; AO verso 12–17
A.M. Blackman, Middle Egyptian Stories, 32, BAe 2, 1932.
J.W.B. Barns, The Ashmolean Ostracon of Sinuhe, 19–20, pl. [7]. London: Oxford University Press for Griffith Institute, 1952.
H. Altenmüller, 'Zur Frage der Mww', 30–1, SAK 2 (1975), 1–37.
A.H. Gardiner, Notes on the Story of Sinuhe, 68–71. Paris: Champion, 1916.

52 Coffin Text Spells 466 and 467
A. de Buck, The Ancient Egyptian Coffin Texts V, 352–62, 363h–366b. (University of Chicago Oriental Institute Publications 73.) Chicago: University of Chicago Press, 1954.
R.O. Faulkner, The Ancient Egyptian Coffin Texts II: Spells 355–787, 93–5. Warminster: Aris & Phillips.
L.H. Lesko, 'The Field of Hetep in Egyptian Coffin Texts', JARCE 9 (1971–2), 89–101.
A. Piankoff, The Wandering of the Soul, 10–11, pl. 1. (Egyptian Religious Texts and Representations, Bollingen Series XI, 6.) Princeton: Princeton University Press, 1974.

53 BM 569
Hieroglyphic Texts from Egyptian Stelae, etc., in the British Museum II, pl. 19–20. London: British Museum, 1912.
J.H. Breasted, Ancient Records of Egypt I: The First to Seventeenth Dynasties, 273–4. Chicago: University of Chicago Press, 1906.
For the cenotaphs see:
D. O'Connor, 'The "Cenotaphs" of the Middle Kingdom at Abydos', in Mélanges Gamal Eddin Mokhtar, II, 161–77, BdE 97, 1985.

54 BM 101
Hieroglyphic Texts from Egyptian Stelae, etc., in the British Museum II, pl. 1–2. London: British Museum, 1912.
A.M. Blackman, 'The Stela of Nebipusenwosret: British Museum No. 101', JEA 21 (1935), 1–9, pl. 1.
J.J. Clère, 'A Note on the Grammatical Gender of the Names of Towns', JEA 23 (1937), 261.
M. Lichtheim, Ancient Egyptian Autobiographies chiefly of the Middle Kingdom: A Study and an Anthology, 122–4, OBO 84 (1988).

55
E. Wente, 'A Misplaced Letter to the Dead', in Miscellanea in honorem Josephi Vergote, Orientalia Lovaniensia Periodica 6/7 (1975/6), 595–600.
E. Brovarski, 'Naga'(Nag')-ed-Der,' LÄ IV, 296–317.

56
A.H. Gardiner and K. Sethe, Egyptian Letters to the Dead: mainly from the Old and Middle Kingdoms, 7, 22, pl. 6. London: Oxford University Press for EES, 1928.

57
W.K. Simpson, 'The Letter to the Dead from the Tomb of Meru (N 3737) at Nag' ed-Deir', JEA 52 (1966), 39–52.
G. Fecht, 'Der Totenbrief von Nag' ed-Deir', MDAIK 24 (1969), 105–28.
C.N. Peck, Some Decorated Tombs of the First Intermediate Period at Naga ed-Der (Brown University doctoral thesis), pl. 13. Ann Arbor: University Microfilms, 1959.

58 P. Harris 500, 6.2–7.3
M.V. Fox, The Song of Songs and the Ancient Egyptian Love Songs, 378–80. Madison: University of Wisconsin Press, 1985.
idem, 'A Study of Antef', Or 46 (1977), 393–423.
J. Bourriau, Pharaohs and Mortals: Egyptian Art in the Middle Kingdom [exhibition catalogue], 76–7, fig. 59. Cambridge: Cambridge University Press, 1988.

59 Graffiti from the tomb of Senet, nos. 1, 3, 29, 33
N. de G. Davies and A.H. Gardiner, The Tomb of Antefoker, Vizier of Sesostris I, and of his Wife, Senet (No. 60), 27–9, pl. 35–7, TTS 2, 1920.
See also:
P.E. Newberry, Beni Hasan I, pl. 38, ASE 1. London: EEF, 1893.
W. Spiegelberg, 'Varia', 98–101, ZÄS 53 (1917), 91–115.

60 P. Chester Beatty IV, 2.5–3.11, 6.11–7.2
A.H. Gardiner, Hieratic Papyri in the British Museum: 3rd series, Chester Beatty Gift, I, 38–41, 43–4, II, pl. 18–9, 20–1. London: British Museum, 1935.